THE CORRECT APP

UNPACKING 'THE SELECT CREED'

THE CORRECT APPROACH TO UNPACKING 'THE SELECT CREED'

Al-Nahjat al-jayyidah li-ḥall alfāẓ Nuqāwat al-ʿaqīdah

Shaykh Muḥammad Nawawī bin ʿUmar al-Jāwī al-Bantanī

Translation & notes by

MUSA FURBER

The Correct Approach to Unpacking 'The Select Creed'
A translation of Shaykh Muḥammad Nawawī bin 'Umar al-Jāwī al-Bantanī's
Al-Nahjat al-jayyidah li-ḥall alfāẓ Nuqāwat al-'aqīdah

Last updated: 20 October 2022.

ISBN 978-1-944904-20-3 (paper)

Published by:
Islamosaic
islamosaic.com
publications@islamosaic.com

Cover image licensed by Ingram Image

بسم الله الرحمن الرحيم

All praise is to Allah alone, the Lord of the Worlds
And may He send His benedictions upon
our master Muhammad, his Kin
and his Companions
and grant them
peace

TRANSLITERATION KEY

ء	' (A distinctive glottal stop made at the bottom of the throat.)
ا	ā, a
ب	b
ت	t
ث	th (Pronounced like the *th* in *think*.)
ج	j
ح	ḥ (A hard *h* sound made at the Adam's apple in the middle of the throat.)
خ	kh (Pronounced like *ch* in Scottish *loch*.)
د	d
ذ	dh (Pronounced like *th* in *this*.)
ر	r (A slightly trilled *r* made behind the upper front teeth.)
ز	z
س	s
ش	sh
ص	ṣ (An emphatic *s* pronounced behind the upper front teeth.)
ض	ḍ (An emphatic *d*-like sound made by pressing the entire tongue against the upper palate.)
ط	ṭ (An emphatic *t* sound produced behind the front teeth.)
ظ	ẓ (An emphatic *th* sound, like the *th* in *this*, made behind the front teeth.)
ع	' (A distinctive Semitic sound made in the middle of the throat and sounding to a Western ear more like a vowel than a consonant.)
غ	gh (A guttural sound made at the top of the throat, resembling the untrilled German and French *r*.)
ف	f
ق	q (A hard *k* sound produced at the back of the palate.)
ك	k
ل	l
م	m
ن	n
ه	h (This sound is like the English *h* but has more body. It is made at the very bottom of the throat and pronounced at the beginning, middle, and ends of words.)
و	ū, u
ي	ī, i, y
ﷺ	A supplication made after mention of the Prophet Muhammad, translated as "May Allah bless him and grant him peace."

CONTENTS

الْمُحْتَوَيَاتُ

TRANSLATOR'S PREFACE

[مُقَدِّمَةُ المُتَرجِمِ]

This book presents Shaykh Muḥammad Nawawī al-Jāwī al-Bantanī's *Al-Nahjah al-jayyidah li-ḥall alfāẓ Nuqāwāt al-ʿaqīdah*, which provides an introduction to essential creed, as well as what is obligatory to believe, know, and perform. Here the Arabic text is presented along with an English translation.

The author of our book is Shaykh Abū ʿAbd al-Muʿṭī Muḥammad Nawawī bin ʿUmar bin ʿArabī bin ʿAlī al-Bantanī al-Jāwī. The last two words in his name refer to him originating from Banten, the westernmost province of the island of Java, in Indonesia. He was born in 1230 AH/1813 CE, in the Tanara district located on the central north coast of Banten, in present day Indonesia. He was a descendent of Sharif Hedayat Allāh, also known as Sunan Gunungjati and one of the "Wali Songo": the nine *awliyā'*, or friends of Allah, who were influential in spreading Islam in the Malay world. Through Sharif Hedayat Allāh, the Shaykh is a descendent of the Prophet ﷺ.

The Shaykh's father and several of his ancestors were also scholars. The Shaykh began his religious studies with his father and then studied with other shaykhs in his region. At the age of 15, he decided to perform Ḥajj. Afterwards, he remained in Mecca an additional three years to study with its scholars. He then returned to Banten. Due to the dismal state of affairs under Dutch colonialism, he soon returned to Mecca. There he spent the rest of his life studying, teaching, and writing.

The Shaykh authored approximately 40 works in various subjects, including creed [*ʿaqīdah*], theology [*kalām*], Quranic exegesis [*tafsīr*], jurisprudence [*fiqh*], principles of jurisprudence [*uṣūl al-fiqh*], and spiritual purification and excellence [*tazkiyah, iḥsān,* and *ṭasawwuf*]. Several of his books spanned multiple subjects (i.e. creed, jurisprudence, and spiritual purification and excellence). Many of his books were published during his lifetime; others remain unpublished. His books were praised by *ʿulamāʾ* in the west as well as in the east.

He is perhaps best known for *Murāḥ labīb,* an exegesis of the Quran; *Qūt al-ḥabīb al-gharīb,* a meta-commentary on Ibn Qāsim al-Ghazzī's *Fatḥ al-qarīb,* itself a commentary on Abū Shujāʿ's conspectus on Shāfiʿī jurisprudence *Ghāyat al-taqrīb*; *Marāqī al-ʿubūdiyyah,* a commentary on Imām al-Ghazālī's *Bidāyat al-hidāyah*; and *Nūr al-ẓallām,* a commentary on Shaykh Aḥmad al-Marzūqī al-Mālikī's versification of creed *ʿAqīdat al-ʿawwām.*

The Shaykh passed away in his home in Mecca, in 1314 AH/ 1879 CE.

The title of our book is *Al-Nahjah al-jayyidah li-ḥall alfāẓ Nuqāwat al-ʿaqīdah,* or *The Correct Approach to Unpacking 'The Select Creed.'* As its title suggests, *Al-Nahjah al-jayyidah* is a commentary on *Nuqāwat al-ʿaqīdah.* The *Nuqāwah* is the author's own introduction to essential creed, and to what is obligatory to believe, know, and perform. The poem consists of 37 lines of verse.

A brief summary of the lines is as follows:

1–2 The opening praise of Allah and blessings upon His Prophet ﷺ.
3 Learning the two testifications of faith (the *shahādatayn*) as the first obligation for all responsible humans.
4–8 What is necessary, impossible and possible for Allah.
9–10 What is necessary, impossible, and possible for the Prophets and Messengers عليهم السلام.
11–15 Various things known only through revelation.
16–18 The first of three supplements concerning matters that are obligatory as beliefs,

19–32 as knowledge,

33–34 and to perform (e.g. the pillars of Islam) or abandon (e.g. blameworthy traits).

35–36 The poem's name and number of its verses.

37 Closing praise of Allah, blessings upon the Prophet ﷺ.

The overall structure and content of the *Nuqāwah* mirrors that of Imām Burhān al-Dīn Ibrāhīm al-Laqqānī's (–1041 AH) versification of basic creed titled *Jawharat al-tawḥīd*. This mirroring suggests a relationship between the *Nuqāwah* and the *Jawharah*. The bulk of *Al-Nahjah al-jayyidah*'s content matches—almost verbatim—Shaykh Ibrāhīm al-Bājūrī's (1197–1276 AH/1784–1860 CE) *Tuḥfat al-murīd*, which is one of the most detailed and popular commentaries for *Jawharat al-tawḥīd*, thus strengthening the hypothesised relationship between our poem and the *Jawharah*. There are also places where material in the *Nahjah* matches (almost verbatim) passages in al-Khaṭīb al-Shirbīnī's Quranic exegesis *Al-Sirāj al-munīr*.

The Shaykh's commentary presents a basic explanation of the *Nuqāwah* appropriate for absolute novices. The explanation tends to lack the evidence and reasoning behind its contents. Those the Shaykh provides in his more advanced works, such as *Fatḥ al-majīd*, a commentary on his teacher Shaykh Aḥmad Ibn al-Sayyid 'Abd al-Raḥmān al-Naḥrāwī's (–1284 AH/–1867 CE) *Al-Durar al-farīd fī 'aqā'id ahl al-tawḥīd*.

I initially translated just the *Nuqāwah*, using the Maṭba'h al-'Āmirah al-'Uthmāniyyah edition of *Al-Nahjah al-jayyidah*, printed in 1303 AH/1889 CE. This edition comprises 17 pages, with the *Nuqāwah* in its margins. I verified my translation of the *Nuqāwah* against a copy of a manuscript (National Library of Ribāṭ, Morocco number 1227). Later, I decided to translate the *Nahjah* as well.

Soon after my initial translation and annotations, Ustaz Zainul Abidin Bin Abdul Halim al-Qadahi published a newer edition of the book (Kajang, Malaysia: Akadimiyyah al-Iḥyā' li-Dirāsat Uṣūl al-Dīn, 2021). Many of the Ustaz's editorial notes on the text confirm what I had found while translating the book; others mention things I had missed. I have included some of his notes on variations between the Ribāṭ manuscript of the *Nuqāwah* (which he denoted with the letter *rā'*) and the earlier printed edition of the *Nahjah* (which he denoted with the letter *'ayn*; I refer to these two as R and A respectively. It is not my intent to provide a critical edition of the book, so readers interested in such an edition of the Arabic text should refer to his. I benefited greatly from conversing with Ustaz Zainul Abidin and have passed these benefits to readers.

I gave references to the relevant verse number in *Jawharat al-tawḥīd* as well as the paragraph number in Shaykh Ali Gomaa's edition of *Tuḥfat al-murīd* (Dār al-Salām); its paragraph numbers allow for a more precise referencing than just the page number, while verse numbers work with in any commentary on the *Jawharah.*

I have also given references for hadiths mentioned explicitly or alluded to in the book. Indexes and online search make it relatively easy to locate hadith texts, so I often limit my referencing to the major hadith collections containing that hadith or to a meta-compendium, such as Imām al-Suyuṭī's *Jāmi' al-aḥādīth.*

I would like to thank the individuals who supported this project. I would also like to thank Anaz Zubair, Hashem Meriesh, Rashad Ali, the Butt family, and Isa Martin for reading through drafts of the book; Abdul Wahab Saleem for his notes on the poem; and Abdul Khafid Mustan and Asif Butt for their help with the cover.

May Allah bless the author of our text Shaykh Muḥammad Nawawī al-Jāwī al-Bantanī, those mentioned in the text or footnotes, those who contributed in any way to bring it to English readers, and their fellow readers. And may He forgive the translator and protect readers from his copious shortcomings.

MUSA FURBER
PUTRAJAYA, MALAYSIA
1444 AH/2022 CE

THE BASIC TEXT

(١) الحَمْدُ لِلَّهِ الَّذِيْ تَوَحَّدَا * ذَاتًا وَأَوْصَافًا كَذَا إِيْجَادَا

(1) **Praise be to Allah who is unified * in essence and attributes and existence**

(٢) ثُمَّ الصَّلَاةُ وَالسَّلَامُ لِلنَّبِيْ * مُحَمَّدٍ وَآلِهِ وَالصَّحْبِ

(2) **Then prayers and blessings for the Prophet * Muḥammad and his folk and Companions**

(٣) وَبَعْدُ فَاجْزِمْ وَاعْتَقِدْ بِالقَلْبِ * مَعْنَى الشَّهَادَتَيْن لِلَّهْ وَالنَّبِيّْ

(3) **To proceed: Be certain and believe in the heart * The meaning of the two testifications to Allah and the Prophet**

(٤) فَاللهُ مَوْجُوْدٌ قَدِيْمٌ بَاقِ * بِذَاتِهِ مُخَالِفٌ لِلْخَلْقِ

(4) **Allah is Existent, Beginningless, Perpetual * In His essence, dissimilar to creation,**

(٥) عَـنْ غَـيْـرِهِ غنِيٌّ وَاحِـدٌ وَحَـيْ * قَـادِرْ بِـقُـدْرَةٍ مُـرِيْـدُ كُـلِّ شَيْ

(5) Free of needing others, One, Living, * All-Able with ability, All-Willing of everything,

(٦) عَالِمْ سَمِيْعٌ وَبَصِيْرٌ بِالبَصَرْ * مُتَكَلِّمٌ بِـلَا شَبَهْ عَلَى البَشَرْ

(6) All-Knowing, All-Hearing, All-Seeing with vision, * Speaking without resembling humanity

(٧) كُـلُّ كَـمَـالٍ وَاجِـبٌ لِـذَاتِـهِ * وَكُـلُّ نَقْصٍ مُمْتَنِعْ فِي حَقِّهِ

(7) Every perfection is necessary for His essence * Every deficiency is impossible for Him

(٨) وَفِعْلُ مُمْكِنْ جَائِزٌ فِي حَقِّهِ * كَـرَزْقِـهِ الخَيْرَ وَبَـعْـثِ رُسْلِـهِ

(8) Performing the possible is permissible for Him * Like His giving good sustenance and sending His messengers

(٩) وَوَاجِـبٌ لَـهُـمْ بَـلَاغٌ صِـدْقُ * وَعِـصْـمَـةٌ مِـمَّا نُـهِـيْ وَحِـذْقُ

(9) Necessary for them are conveying, truthfulness, * Preservation from committing what is forbidden and intelligence

(١٠) وَضِـدَّهَـا نَـزِّهْ كَـكُـلِّ قَـادِحْ * وَغَـيْـرُهُ يَـجُـوْزُ مِـنْ أَكْـلٍ نِكَاحْ

(10) **Declare [them] free from their opposites (like all that impugns). * And others are permissible (including eating and marriage)**

(١١) وَوَاجِـبٌ إِيْمَانُنَا بِالمُرْسَلِيْنْ * وَالأَنْـبِـيَا وَكُـتُـبٍ وَالكَاتِبِيْنْ

(11) **Our belief in the messengers is obligatory * And the prophets, books, and the [angelic] scribes**

(١٢) وَالبَعْثِ وَالحَوْضِ وَبِالحِسَابِ * وَالـوَزْنِ وَالـصِّـرَاطِ وَالكِـتَابِ

(12) **And [in] the resurrection, the watering pool, and accounting * And the scale, the bridge, and the book**

(١٣) وَالـعَـرْشِ وَالكُرْسِيِّ وَالشَّفَاعَةْ * لَـوْحٍ قَـلَـمْ وَبَـرْزَخٍ نَـعِـيْـمَـهْ

(13) **And the throne, and the stool, and the intercession, * Tablet, pen, *barzakh,* blissfulness**

(١٤) عَـذَابِـهِ وَجَـنَّـةٍ نِـيْـرَانِ * وَالـحُـوْرِ وَالـقُـصُـوْرِ وَالـوِلْـدَانِ

(14) **Its torment, and paradise, fire * The houris, the palaces, and the youths**

(١٥) وَوَاجِــبٌ إِيْـمَـانُـنَـا بِـالـقَـدَرِ * وَبِـالـقَـضَـا بِـالـنَّـفْـعِ وَبِـالـضَّـرَرِ

(15) **Our belief in destiny is obligatory * And in the decree, in benefit and in harm,**

(١٦) ثُمَّ اعْتَقِدْ أَنَّ الخَلَائِقْ فِعْلَهَا * مَـخْـلُـوْقَـةٌ لِـلَّـهِ لَا تَـزِغْ لَهَا

(16) **Then believe that created beings—their actions * Are created by Allah, so do not stray because of it**

(١٧) رُؤْيَـةَ مَوْلَى ثَـمَّ إِسْـرَاءَ النَّبِيْ * بَـــرَاءَةً لِعَـائِـشَـةْ مِـنْ كَـذِبِ

(17) **Seeing our Lord during the Night Journey of our Prophet, * The innocence of 'Ā'ishah from lies**

(١٨) وَأَفْـضَـلُ الـخَـلْـقِ مُـحَـمَّـدٌ بِـهِ * خَـتْـمُ رُسُـلْ وَعَـمَّ فِـيْ بِعْثَتِهِ

(18) **The best of creation is Muḥammad, through him * He sealed the messengers and universalised his sending**

(١٩) ثُمَّ اعْرِفِ الخَمْسَ وَعِشْرِيْنَ وَهُمْ * آدَمْ وَإِدْرِيْـــسُ وَنُـــوْحٌ هُـوْدُ ثُمْ

(19) **Then know the twenty-five [prophets] and they are * Ādam, Idrīs, and Nūḥ, Hūd, and then**

(٢٠) صَالِحْ وَإِبْرَاهِيْمُ لُوْطٌ وَكَذَا * إِسْحَاقُ إِسْمَاعِيْلُ يَعْقُوْبُ احْتَذَى

(20) Ṣāliḥ, and Ibrāhīm, Lūṭ, and likewise * Isḥāq, Ismā'īl, Ya'qūb followed

(٢١) يُوْسُفْ وَأَيُّوْبُ شُعَيْبٌ مُوْسَى * هَارُوْنُ وَالْيَسَعْ وَذُو الكِفْلِ عَسَا

(21) Yūsuf, and Ayyūb, Shu'ayb, Mūsā * Hārūn, and al-Yasa' and Dhu al-Kifl (who toughened)

(٢٢) دَاوُدُ نَجْلُهُ سُلَيْمَانُ اسْتَوَى * إِلْيَاسُ يُوْنُسْ زَكَرِيَّا يَحْيَى

(22) Dāwūd, his offspring Sulaymān was firm and steady * Ilyās, Yūnus, Zakariyyā, Yaḥyā

(٢٣) عِيْسَى مُحَمَّدٌ عَلَيْهِمُ السَّلَامْ * مِنَ الرَّحِيْمِ مَا بَقَى الأَيَّامْ[1]

(23) 'Īsā, Muḥammad upon whom be peace * From the Most Merciful so long as days remain

(٢٤) ثُمَّ اعْرِفِ العَشَرَةَ بِالتَّحْقِيْقِ * جِبْرِيْلُ مِيْكَائِلُ قَاسِمْ رِزْقِ

(24) Then know the ten [angels] in detail * Jībrīl, Mīkā'īl the divider of sustenance,

1 This is as it is in A and R have. Ustaz Zainul Abidin suggests «مِنَ الرَّحِيْمِ مَا بَقِيْ مِنَ الأَيَّامْ», though «مِنَ الرَّحِيْمِ مَا تَبَقَّى الأَيَّامْ» is also better.

(٢٥) فِي اللَّوْحِ إِسْرَافِيْلُ عَزْرَائِيْلُ * رِضْوَانُ مَالِكٌ رَقِيْبُ الكَامِلُ

(25) **In the Tablet, Isrāfīl, ʿAzrā'īl, * Riḍwān, Mālik, Raqīb the complete**

(٢٦) عَتِيْدُ مُنْكَرْ وَنَكِيْرْ قَبْلَهُمَا * رُوْمَانُ نَاكُوْرٌ فَقِيْلَ مَعْهُمَا

(26) **ʿAtīd, Munkar, and Nakīr before them both * Rūmān, Nākūr, and it's said [he's] with them both**

(٢٧) وَاعْرِفْ صُحُفْ مُوْسَى وَإِبْرَاهِيْمْ[2] كَذَا * تَوْرَاةُ إِنْجِيْلٌ زَبُوْرٌ فَاحْتَذَى

(27) **Know the scriptures of Mūsā, and Ibrāhīm likewise, * Torah, Gospels, and Psalms, following**

(٢٨) قُرْآنُ ثُمَّ غَيْرُهَا بِالجُمْلَةِ * وَاعْرِفْ لِأَنْسَابِ النَّبِيْ وَصُوْرَةِ

(28) **Quran, then others in general * And know the lineage of the Prophet and [his] appearance**

(٢٩) وَأَوْلَادُهُ[3] قَاسِمْ وَزَيْنَبٌ أَتَتْ * رُقَيَّةٌ وَفَاطِمَةْ قَدِ احْتَذَتْ

(29) **And [his] children Qāsim, and Zaynab arrived * Ruqayyah, and Fāṭimah she followed**

---

2 This is as all editions have it, though «أَبْرَهَمْ» would be better for the metre.

3 This is as all editions have it, though starting with «أَولَادُهُ» would be better for the metre.

(٣٠) وَأُمُّ كَلْثُوْمٍ وَعَبْدُ اللهِ ثُمَّ * إِبْرَاهِيْمٌ مِنْ مَارِيَةْ فَادْرِ وَرُمْ

(30) **Umm Kalthūm, and 'Abd Allāh then * Ibrāhīm from Māriyah so be cognisant of them**

(٣١) وَاعْرِفْ خَصَائِصَ النَّبِيْ مِنْ وَاجِبَةْ * مُحَرَّمٍ تَخْفِيْفَةٍ فَضِيْلَةْ

(31) **The best known matters exclusive to the Prophet are obligatory, * unlawful, lightened, or a superior quality**

(٣٢) وِلِإِقَامِ الدِّيْنِ كَالطَّهَارَةِ * وَالصَّوْمِ وَالصَّلَاةِ وَالزَّكَاةِ

(32) **And [knowing what is obligatory] to uphold the religion, like purification * And fasting, and prayer, and zakat**

(٣٣) وَاعْمَلْ بِتَقْلِيْدِ إِمَامٍ ثُمَّا * حِفْظٍ لِكُلِّيَّاتٍ ثُمَّ تَمِّمَا

(33) **Act by emulating an Imām then * Preserving the universal [obligations], then finish up**

(٣٤) بِتَرْكِ تَسْمِيْعٍ وَعُجْبٍ كِبْرٍ * رِيَا حَسَدٍ[4] اغْتِيَابِ غَيْرِ

(34) **By ceasing from telling of one's works, and pride, arrogance, * Showing off, envy, backbiting, talebearing others**

4 A adds «نَمِيْمَةٍ» after this. Unfortunately, its inclusion breaks the metre.

(٣٥) سَمَّيْتُهَا نُقَاوَةَ العَقِيْدَةْ * أَبْيَاتُهَا لَوْ يَنْبَغِي[5] أَنْ تُقْصَدَهْ

(35) I named it "The Select Creed," * Its verses ought to be sought

(٣٦) تَارِيْخُهَا غَرْقٌ فَيَا رَبِّ الْطُفِ * بِنَا وَوَالِدٍ عَقِبٍ وَاسْعَفِ

(36) Its history is "*gharq*," so, O Lord, be gentle * To us, and parents, progeny, and give aid

(٣٧) وَالحَمْدُ لِلَّهْ صَلِّ سَلِّمْ لِلنَّبِيْ[6] * وَالآلِ وَالصَّحْبِ أُوْلِي المَنَاقِبِ

(37) Praise to Allah, pray and bless the Prophet * And the folk and Companions with the most virtues.

---

5 All editions have «لو ينبغي». Perhaps «جَدِيْرَةٌ» would be better linguistically and for the metre.

6 Perhaps «على النَّبِيْ» would be better linguistically.

INTRODUCTION TO THE COMMENTARY

[مُقَدِّمَةُ الشَّرحِ]

(بِسْمِ اللَّهِ الرَّحْمَنِ الرَّحِيْمِ)

In the name of Allah the Most Merciful and Compassionate

الحَمْـدُ لِلَّـهِ المُنْفَـرِدِ بِالإِعْدَامِ وَالإِيْجَـادِ، المُنَزَّهِ عَنْ النَّقَائِصِ وَالأَشْـبَاهِ وَالأَنْدَادِ، وَأَشْهَدُ أَنْ لَا إِلَهَ إِلَّا اللَّهُ المُخَالِفِ لِلكَائِنَاتِ، البَاقِي وَكُلُّ مَنْ عَدَاهُ هَالِكٌ مِنَ المَخْلُوْقَاتِ. وَأَشْـهَدُ أَنَّ سَـيِّدَنَا مُحَمَّدًا رَسُوْلُهُ الصَّادِقُ الأَمِيْـنُ ذُوْ المَـدَدِ الأَنْمَـى فِي كُلِّ حِيْنَ، صَلَّى اللَّهُ عَلَيْهِ وَسَـلَّمَ صَلَاةً وَسَلَامًا فَضْلَهُمَا مِدْرَارٌ، وَعَلَى آلِهِ وَصَحْبِهِ وَالتَّابِعِيْنَ إِلَى يَوْمِ القَرَارِ.

Praise is to Allah who is singled out with bringing [things] into non-existence and existence; who transcends deficiencies, resemblances, and equals. I testify that there is no deity except Allah, independent of all contingent entities [*kā'ināt*]. He endures and everything except Him are perishing created beings. I testify that our master Muḥammad is His messenger, the truthful and trustworthy, possessor of the most expansive aid in all instances of time. May Allah shower him in prayers and blessings, and upon his folk and companions and followers until the [final] decisive day.

أَمَّا بَعْدُ، فَيَقُوْلُ كَثِيْرُ الذَّنْبِ وَالمَسَاوِي مُحَمَّدٌ نَوَوِيٌّ الجَاوِيُّ: هَذَا شَرْحٌ عَلَى مَنْظُوْمَتِي فِي التَّوْحِيْدِ، سَمَّيْتُهُ «النَّهْجَةَ الجَيِّدَةَ لِحَلِّ أَلْفَاظِ نُقَاوَةِ العَقِيْدَةِ» جَعَلَهُ اللَّهُ تَعَالَى خَالِصًا لِوَجْهِهِ وَنَافِعًا لِمَنْ يَشْتَغِلُ بِتَعَلُّمِهِ وَتَعْلِيْمِهِ. وَاللهَ تَعَالَى أَسْأَلُ وَبِنَبِيِّهِ أَتَوَسَّلُ أَنْ يَغْفِرَ لِي وَلِوَالِدَيَّ وَلِأَحْبَابِي. وَهَا أَنَا أَشْرَعُ فِي المَقْصُوْدِ فَأَقُوْلُ وَعَلَى اللهِ التَّوَكُّلُ فِي الإِعَانَةِ لِلإِتْمَامِ وَالصَّوَابِ إِنَّهُ خَيْرُ مَرْجُوٍ وَمَأْمُوْلٍ وَأَكْرَمُ مَقْصُوْدٍ وَمَسْؤُوْلٍ

To precede: He of many sins and wretchednesss, Muḥammad Nawawī al-Jāwī, says:

This is a commentary on my poem concerning monotheistic creed [*al-tawḥīd*]; I named it *Al-Nahjat al-jayyidah li-ḥall alfāẓ Nuqāwat al-ʿaqīdah*.

May Allah (Most High is He) make it purely for His pleasure, and beneficial to whomever busies himself with studying and teaching it. I ask Allah (Most High is He) [alone] and beseech [Him] through His messenger that He forgives me, my parents, and those I love.

And now I begin the intended [matter], so I say (and [my] reliance is upon Allah for assistance in completing it and it being correct, since He is the best that can be hoped and wished for, the noblest of goals and asked of [and for]):

INTRODUCTION TO THE BASIC TEXT

[مُقَدِّمَةُ النَّظمِ]

(بِسْمِ اللَّهِ الرَّحْمَنِ الرَّحِيْمِ)

In the name of Allah the Most Merciful and Compassionate

أَي: أُنَظِّمُ. وَإِنَّمَا لَمْ يَأْتِ النَّاظِمُ بِالتَّسْمِيَّةِ نَظْمًا لِأَنَّهُ خِلَافُ الأَوْلَى؛ لِأَنَّهُ لَمْ يَجِئْ عَلَى صِيْغَةِ التَّسْمِيَّةِ الَّتِي فِي القُرْآنِ الكَرِيْمِ.

Meaning: I versify [in the name of Allah the Most Merciful and Compassionate]. The versifier did not bring the *Basmalah* in verse [form] because it would be suboptimal since it would not have come with the form of the *Basmalah* that is in the Noble Quran.

(١) الحَمْدُ لِلَّهِ الَّذِيْ تَوَحَّدَا * ذَاتًا وَأَوْصَافًا كَذَا إِيْجَادَا

(1) Praise be to Allah who is unified * in essence and attributes and existence

أَي: أَصِفُهُ تَعَالَى بِجَمِيْعِ الكَمَالَاتِ الَّتِي وَصَفَ بِهَا نَفْسَهُ حَيْثُ وَصَفَ. وَافْتَتَحَ النَّاظِمُ كِتَابَهُ بِالبَسْمَلَةِ ثُمَّ الحَمْدَلَةِ اقْتِدَاءً بِالكِتَابِ العَظِيْمِ فِي ابْتِدَائِهِ بِهِمَا.

Meaning: I describe Him Most High with all of the perfections with which He described Himself when He has done so.

The versifier began his writing with "In the name of Allah the Most Merciful and Compassionate," then "Praise be to Allah," out of following the example of the Magnificent Book [i.e. the Quran] in it beginning with the two.[7]

(٢) ثُمَّ الصَّلَاةُ وَالسَّلَامُ لِلنَّبِيْ * مُحَمَّدٍ وَآلِهِ وَالصَّحْبِ

(2) Then prayers and blessings for the Prophet * Muḥammad and his folk and Companions

لَمَّا حَمِدَ النَّاظِمُ اللَّهَ تَعَالَى صَلَّى عَلَى نَبِيِّهِ ﷺ بِقَوْلِهِ تَعَالَى: ﴿وَرَفَعْنَا لَكَ ذِكْرَكَ﴾ أَي: لَا أُذْكَرُ إِلَّا وَتُذْكَرُ مَعِي. وَإِنَّمَا ذَكَرَ «الآلَ»(8) لِلنَّهْيِ عَنِ الصَّلَاةِ البَتْرَاءِ؛ وَهِيَ الَّتِي لَمْ يُذْكَرْ فِيهَا الآلُ. وَإِنَّمَا ذَكَرَ «الصَّحْبَ» مَعَ دُخُولِهِمْ فِي الآلِ - بِالمَعْنَى الأَعَمِّ، وَهُوَ كُلُّ مُؤْمِنٍ - لِمَزِيدِ الاهْتِمَامِ.

After the versifier has praised Allah (Most High is He), he offered prayers and blessings upon His prophet ﷺ in accordance with Him Most High saying, "And exalted your repute,"[9] i.e. "I am not mentioned save that you are mentioned with Me."

He [the versifier] mentioned "folk" because of the prohibition of

7 Al-Laqqānī, *Jawharat al-tawḥīd* (printed within *Tuḥfat al-murīd*), introduction (line zero); al-Bayjūrī, *Tuḥfat al-murīd* (Cairo: Dār al-Salām, 2002/1422), paragraph #3. For the sake of brevity, further references will be shortened to "*Jawharah*" followed by a line number, and "*Tuḥfah*" followed by a paragraph number, e.g. *Jawharah*, 4; *Tuḥfah*, 45.

8 Ustaz Zainul Abidin mentioned that A has «الأول», and perhaps what is mentioned here is better.

9 Al-Sharḥ, 94:4.

the "amputated prayer [*al-ṣalāt al-batrā'*],"[10] which is a supplication in which the folk are not mentioned.

He mentioned the "companions" even though they fall within the more general meaning of "folk" (which is every believer[11]) in order to increase its importance.[12]

THE FIRST OBLIGATION FOR RESPONSIBLE INDIVIDUALS [أَوَّلُ واجِبٍ على المُكَلَّفِ]

(٣) وَبَعْدُ فَاجْزِمْ وَاعْتَقِدْ بِالقَلْبِ * مَعْنَى الشَّهَادَتَيْنِ لِلَّهْ وَالنَّبِيّْ

(3) To proceed: Be certain and believe in the heart * The meaning of the two testifications to Allah and the Prophet

أَي: أَوَّلُ وَاجِبٍ عَلَى المُكَلَّفِ تَعَلُّمُ كَلِمَتَي الشَّهَادَةِ وَفَهْمُ مَعْنَاهُمَا. وَهُوَ قَوْلُ «لَا إِلَهَ إِلَّا اللَّهُ مُحَمَّدٌ رَسُوْلُ اللَّهِ». وَيَكْفِي أَنْ يُصَدِّقَ ثُبُوْتَ الأُلُوْهِيَّةِ لِلَّهِ تَعَالَى وَانْتِفَائَهَا عَنْ غَيْرِهِ تَعَالَى، وَثُبُوْتَ الرِّسَالَةِ لِسَيِّدِنَا مُحَمَّدٍ ﷺ بِحَيْثُ يَعْتَقِدُ ذَلِكَ جَزْمًا مِنْ غَيْرِ اخْتِلَاجِ رَيْبٍ وَاضْطِرَابِ نَفْسٍ. وَقَدْ يَحْصُلُ ذَلِكَ بِمُجَرَّدِ التَّقْلِيْدِ وَالسَّمَاعِ مِنْ غَيْرِ بَحْثٍ وَلَا بُرهَانٍ.

The first duty[13] for a responsible individual[14] is to learn the two phrases of the testification of faith [Ar. *al-shahādah*] and to under-

---

10 *Jawharah*, 4; *Tuḥfah*, 45.
11 *Jawharah*, 4; *Tuḥfah*, 45.
12 *Jawharah*, 4; *Tuḥfah*, 46.
13 *Jawharah*, 14; *Tuḥfah*, 95.
14 *Jawharah*, 9; *Tuḥfah*, 68–69. There it clarifies that a responsible human being is one who is mature, rational, has been reached by the call to Islam, and whose senses are sound.

stand their meaning. The testification is saying: "There is no deity except Allah, Muḥammad is the Messenger of Allah" ("*lā ilāha illa Llāhu, Muḥammadun rasūlu Llāh*"). It suffices that one believes[15] in the divinity of Allah (Most High is He) while negating it [this divinity] from anything other than Him Most High, and [that one believes in] the messenger-hood of our master Muḥammad ﷺ such that one believes it with conviction and without being troubled by doubts or confusion. This may be achieved by simply emulating another's opinion [*al-taqlīd*] and through heeding it without it being accompanied by contemplation [*naẓr*] or proof [*burhān*].[16]

أَي: أَوَّلُ وَاجِبٍ نَافِعٍ فِي الدَّارَيْنِ النُّطْقُ بِكَلِمَةِ التَّوْحِيْدِ مَعَ التَّصْدِيْقِ بِمَضْمُوْنِهَا كَمَا قَالَ رَسُوْلُ اللهِ ﷺ لِمُعَاذٍ لَمَّا بَعَثَهُ إِلَى اليَمَنِ: «إِنَّكَ تَقْدَمُ عَلَى قَوْمٍ مِنْ أَهْلِ الكِتَابِ، فَلْيَكُنْ أَوَّلُ مَا تَدْعُوْهُمْ إِلَى أَنْ يُوَحِّدُوْا اللَّهَ»، وَفِي رِوَايَةٍ: «إِلَى عِبَادَةِ اللَّهِ» «فَإِذَا عَرَفُوْا اللَّهَ فَأَخْبِرْهُمْ أَنْ اللَّهَ قَدْ فَرَضَ عَلَيْهِمْ خَمْسَ صَلَوَاتٍ». قَالَ بَعْضُهُمْ: «المُرَادُ بِالمَعْرِفَةِ الإِقْرَارُ وَالطَّوَاعِيَةُ» أهـ.

So: The first duty that is beneficial in the two abodes [i.e. this life and the afterlife] is uttering the phrase of monotheism [*kalimat al-tawḥīd*] while believing its contents to be true[17]—just as the Messenger of Allah ﷺ said to Mu'ādh [رضي الله عنه] when dispatching him to Yemen: "You will come upon a group from the People of the Book [i.e. Jews, Christians, others who received revelation]. The first thing you should call them to is to declare the unicity of Allah..."—another version [of the report] has: "...to worship Allah..."—"...And if they know Allah, inform them that Allah has made five prayers incumbent upon them."[18]

15 cf *Jawharah*, 18; *Tuḥfah*, 114.
16 *Jawharah*, 11, 13, 14; *Tuḥfah*, 82, 93, 95.
17 *Jawharah*, 18, 19; *Tuḥfah*, 117, 120.
18 Al-Bukhārī, 1458, 7372; Muslim, 31 #19.

Some [of the *'ulamā'*] are of the opinion that what is intended by "knowing" [in this hadith] is to declare [believe in Allah's unicity] and obey it.[19]

أَمَّـا النُّطْـقُ بِـ«لَا إِلَهَ إِلَّا اللهُ» مُجَرَّدًا عَنِ التَّصْدِيْقِ؛ فَإِنَّمَا يَنْفَعُ فِي الدُّنْيَا مَا لَمْ نَطَّلِعْ عَلَى كُفْرِهِ بِعَلَامَةٍ كَسُـجُوْدٍ لِصَنَمٍ، وَإِلَّا جَرَتْ عَلَيْهِ أَحْكَامُ الكُفْرِ،

As for uttering, "There is no deity except for Allah" ("*lā ilāha illa Llāhu*") decoupled from believing it to be true: It is only beneficial [to the one who says it] in this life [the *dunyā*] so long as we do not observe his disbelief through an indicator, such as prostrating to an idol. Otherwise, the rulings of disbelief will apply to him [i.e. in this life as well as in the afterlife].

وَأَمَّـا مُجَـرَّدُ التَّصْدِيْـقِ؛ فَإِنْ لَـمْ يَكُنْ تَـرْكُ النُّطْقِ بِذَلِكَ عَنْ إِبَـاءَةٍ بَعْدَ المُطَالَبَـةِ فَهُـوَ نَافِعٌ فِـي الآخِرَةِ فَقَطْ. وَذَلِكَ أَنَّ فِـي المُكَلَّفِيْنَ مِنْ غَيْرِ العَرَبِ مَنْ لَا يُحسِـنُ النُّطْقَ بِكَلِمَتَيِ الشَّـهَادَةِ وَلَا يَفْهَمُ مَعْنَاهُمَا. فَإِذَا بَلَغَتْـهُ الدَّعْـوَةُ فَأَوَّلُ وَاجِـبٍ عَلَيْهِ تَعَلُّمُهُمَا وَفَهْمُ مَعْنَاهُمَـا لِيُمْكِنَهُ الإِقْرَارُ بِهِمَا مُصَدِّقًا بِمَضْمُوْنِهِمَا، فَإِنَّهُ وَسِيْلَةٌ إِلَى مَا هُوَ المَقْصُوْدُ بِالذَّاتِ؛ وَهُوَ إِثْبَاتُ كُلِّ كَمَالٍ لِلَّهِ تَعَالَى وَنَفْيُ كُلِّ نَقْصٍ عَنْهُ تَعَالَى، وَإِثْبَاتُ مَا يَجِبُ لِلرَّسُوْلِ مِنَ الصِّفَاتِ وَمَا أَخْبَرَهُ وَنَفْيُ مَا يَقْدَحُ لَهُ فِي مَرَاتِبِهِ.

As for simply believing it to be true [i.e. "There is no deity except for Allah" decoupled from its utterance]: If omitting its utterance is not an act of refusal after one has been [rightfully] required [to state it], then it [i.e. believing it without uttering it] is of benefit

19 For this last opinion and the source for the comments between brackets: Ibn Ḥajar, *Fatḥ al-Bārī*, 13:354. For these last two paragraphs: *Jawharah*, 18, 19; *Tuḥfah*, 117, 120.

only in the afterlife.[20] This is because responsible individuals [as a class] includes non-Arabs who are not able to correctly pronounce the two phrases of the testification of faith and do not understand its meaning. Consequently, if the call [to Islam] reaches one [of them], his first duty is to learn the two [testifications] and to understand their meaning in order to enable him to declare them while assenting to their contents.

For it [declaring them while assenting to their truth] is a means to what is the essential objective: Affirming every perfection to Allah (Most High is He) and negating every deficiency from Him Most High; and affirming the attributes that are obligatory for the Messenger and [affirming] what he has informed [us], and negating whatever impugns his rank.

وَلَا بُدَّ لِمَنْ يُرِيْدُ الدُّخُوْلَ فِي الإِسْلَامِ مِنْ أَنْ يَنْطِقَ بِالشَّهَادَتَيْنِ، وَمِنْ لَفْظِ «أَشْهَدُ» وَتَكْرِيْرِهِ. وَلَا يَكْفِي ابْدَالُ لَفْظِ «أَشْهَدُ» بِغَيْرِهِ.

Someone who intends to enter Islam must utter the two testifications of faith, must pronounce [the phrase] "I testify [*ashhadu*]," and must repeat it. [Thus, he says: "*ashhadu an lā ilāha illa Llāh, ashhadu anna Muḥammadan rasūlu Llāh.*"]

It does not suffice to replace "I testify [*ashhadu*]" with something else.[21]

MEANING OF THE TWO TESTIFICATIONS OF FAITH [مَعنى الشَّهادَتَينِ]

فَمَعْنَى «أَشْهَدُ أَنْ لَا إِلَهَ إِلَّا اللهُ» أَي: أُقِرُّ بِاللِّسَانِ وَأُصَدِّقُ بِالقَلْبِ أَنَّهُ

20 *Jawharah*, 19; *Tuḥfah*, 120.
21 *Jawharah*, 18; *Tuḥfah*, 117.

لَا مُسْتَحِقًّا لِلعِبَادَةِ فِي الوَاقِعِ مَوْجُوْدٌ إِلَّا اللَّهُ، فَانْسُبُ اللَّهَ تَعَالَى إِلَى الوَحْدَانِيَّةِ فِي أُلُوْهِيَّتِهِ.

The meaning of "I testify that there is no deity except Allah [*ashhadu an lā ilāha illa Llāh*]" is "I declare with my tongue and I believe in my heart to be true that nothing that actually exists is deserving of worship except Allah, and I thus ascribe to Allah's uniqueness in His divinity.[22]

وَمَعْنَى «أَشْهَدُ أَنَّ مُحَمَّدًا رَسُوْلُ اللهِ» أَي: أُقِرُّ بِاللِّسَانِ وَأُصَدِّقُ بِالقَلْبِ أَنَّ مُحَمَّدًا رَسُوْلُ اللهِ لِلخَلْقِ كَافَّةً، فَانْسُبُ الرِّسَالَةَ لِسَيِّدِنَا مُحَمَّدٍ ﷺ.

The meaning of "I testify that Muḥammad is the Messenger of Allah [*ashhadu anna Muḥammadan rasūlu Llāh*]" is "I declare with my tongue and believe in my heart that Muḥammad is the Messenger of Allah to all of the creatures, and I thus ascribe messenger-hood to our master Muḥammad ﷺ."

THE PROPHET ﷺ WAS SENT TO ALL OF CREATION [بعثة النَّبيِّ ﷺ لِلخَلقِ كافَّة]

وَهُوَ مَبْعُوْثٌ إِلَى كُلِّ خَلْقٍ حَتَّى الحَيَوَانَاتِ وَالنَّبَاتَاتِ وَالجَمَادَاتِ؛ فَإِنَّ كُلَّ مَخْلُوْقٍ حَيٌّ عَالِمٌ -وَإِنْ تَفَاوَتَتْ رَوَاتِبُ حَيَاتِهَا وَإِدْرَاكَاتِهَا- فَصَحَّ أَنْ يُكَلَّفَ تَكْلِيْفًا بِحَسَبِ حَالِهِ[23]. فَإِنَّ الإِنْسَانَ المُكَلَّفَ يَخْتَلِفُ تَكْلِيْفُ أَفْرَادِهِ بِحَسَبِ اخْتِلَافِ أَحْوَالِهِمْ فِي الوُسْعِ[24] اخْتِيَارًا وَاضْطِرَارًا فَيُبَاحُ لِهَذَا مَا يُحَرَّمُ عَلَى ذَاكَ، وَعَلَى هَذَا فَقِسْ بَقِيَّةَ الأَحْكَامِ، وَفِي

22 cf *Jawharah*, 63; *Tuḥfah*, 427–35 (esp. 435).

23 Ustaz Zainul Abidin mentioned that the author would sometimes mix masculine pronouns with feminine antecedents, and vice versa—as is happening here.

24 Ustaz Zainul Abidin mentioned that A has «الواسع», and perhaps what is mentioned here is better since it matches what is in its source.

الحَدِيْثِ: «مَا صِيْدَ صَيْدٌ، وَلَا عُضِدَتْ عَضَاةٌ وَلَا قُطِعَتْ وَشِيْجَةٌ إِلَّا بِقِلَّةِ التَّسْبِيْحِ». وَهَذَا يَدُلُّ عَلَى أَنَّ التَّكْلِيْفَ لِسَائِرِ الأَشْيَاءِ كَثْرَةُ(25) التَّسْبِيْحِ فَمَنْ قَصُرَ فِيْمَا كُلِّفَ بِهِ جُوْزِيَ بِمَا يَقْتَضِيهِ العَدْلُ الإِلَهِيُّ، وَيَعْفُوْ عَنْ كَثِيْرٍ.

He [ﷺ] was sent to all creatures—even animals, plants, and inanimate objects.[26] [This is] because every created being is alive and cognisant (even if they differ in the degrees of their lives and perceptions), and thus it is valid for them to be held responsible in accordance with their condition. Indeed, the responsibility of responsible human beings differs in accordance with their capacities [for] voluntary and involuntary [acts]. Thus, what is permissible to one is unlawful to another. (One is to draw analogies from this for all other rulings.) [There is evidence] in the [following] hadith: "No prey was caught, no thorny tree felled, and no root severed except due to the small quantity of glorifying Allah [*tasbīḥ*]."[27] This [hadith] indicates that all other things have a responsibility to glorify Allah abundantly, and whoever is negligent in their responsibility will be recompensed with whatever divine justice calls for. And He excuses a lot!

THE SUBJECTS OF THEOLOGY [مَباحِثُ فَنِّ العَقِيدَةِ]

وَاعْلَمْ أَنَّ مَبَاحِثَ هَذَا الفَنِّ ثَلَاثَةُ أَقْسَامٍ: الإِلَهِيَّاتُ وَهِيَ المَسَائِلُ المَبْحُوْثُ فِيْهَا عَمَّا يَجِبُ لِلَّهِ تَعَالَى وَمَا يَسْتَحِيْلُ عَلَيْهِ وَمَا يَجُوْزُ فِي

25 Ustaz Zainul Abidin mentioned that A has «كثيرة», and perhaps what is mentioned here is better since it matches what is in its source.

26 *Jawharah*, 3; *Tuḥfah*, 34.

27 Ibn Ḥajar al-ʿAsqalānī, *Al-Maṭālib al-ʿāliyah*, 3405; Jalāl al-Dīn al-Suyūṭī, *Jamʿ al-jawāmiʿ*, 19005/509; cf al-Suyūṭī, *Al-Jāmiʿ al-ṣaghīr*, 11873. Its chain is very weak.

حَقِّهِ، وَنُبُوَّيَّاتُ وَهِيَ المَسَائِلُ المَبْحُوثُ فِيهَا عَمَّا يَجِبُ لِلرُّسُلِ وَمَا

يَسْتَحِيْلُ عَلَيْهِمْ وَمَا يَجُوزُ فِي حَقِّهِمْ.

Know that the subjects of this art are in three sections:

1 *Matters related to the Divine* [al-ilāhiyyāt] (the issues which study what is obligatory for Allah, what is impossible for Him, and what is permissible for Him),
2 *Matters related to the prophets* [al-nubuwwiyyāt] (the issues which study what is obligatory for the messengers, what is impossible for them, and what is permissible for them)[; and
3 *Revealed Matters* [al-sam'iyyāt] (the issues which can be known only through revelation)].[28]

NECESSARY, IMPOSSIBLE, AND PERMISSIBLE   [الواجِبُ وَالمُستَحِيلُ وَالجَائِزُ]

وَالوَاجِبُ مَا لَا يَقْبَلُ الإِنْتِفَاءَ، وَالمُسْتَحِيْلُ مَا لَا يَقْبَلُ الثُّبُوْتَ، وَالجَائِزُ

مَا يَقْبَلُ الثُّبُوْتَ تَارَةً وَالاِنْتِفَاءَ تَارَةً أُخْرَى.

[The words "necessary," "impossible," and "permissible" have a technical meaning in this subject.]

Necessary [wājib] is what does not accept being negated.[29]

Impossible [mustaḥīl] is what does not accept being affirmed.

Permissible [jā'iz] is what accepts being affirmed sometimes and negated other times.[30]

---

28 The third is not listed here in the Arabic, but it is mentioned later on in the book and it is a standard section. *Jawharah*, 23; *Tuḥfah*, 139.
29 *Jawharah*, 9; *Tuḥfah*, 77.
30 For these two: *Jawharah*, 10; *Tuḥfah*, 78–79.

1

MATTERS RELATED TO THE DIVINE

[قِسْمُ الإلهِيَّاتِ]

وَقَدْ بَدَأْتُ بِالإِلَهِيَّاتِ لِأَنَّهَا أَشْرَفُ الأَقْسَامِ، فَقُلْتُ:

I began with matters related to the Divine because it is the noblest division.[31] I said:

WHAT IS NECESSARY AND IMPOSSIBLE FOR HIM (MOST HIGH IS HE)

[ما يَجِبُ في حَقِّهِ تَعالى وَما يَستَحيلُ]

(٤) فَـالله مَـوْجُـوْدٌ قَـدِيْـمٌ بَـاقِ * بِـذَاتِـهِ مُـخَـالِـفٌ لِلْخَـلْقِ

(4) **Allah is Existent, Beginningless, Everlastingness * In His essence, dissimilarity to creation,**

(٥) عَـنْ غَـيْـرِهِ غَنِيٌّ وَاحِـدٌ وَحَـيْ * قَـادِرٌ بِقُـدْرَةٍ مُـرِيْـدُ كُـلِّ شَيْ

(5) **Free of needing others, One, Living, * All-Able with ability, All-Willing of everything,**

---

31 *Jawharah*, 23; *Tuḥfah*, 139.

(٦) عَالِمْ سَمِيْعٌ وَبَصِيْرٌ بِالبَصَرْ * مُتَكَلِّمٌ بِلَا شَبَهْ عَلَى البَشَرْ

(6) All-Knowing, All-Hearing, All-Seeing with vision, * Speaking without resembling humanity

ذَكَرَ النَّاظِمُ ثَلَاثَةَ عَشَرَةَ(32) صِفَةً بِذِكْرِ الأَسْمَاءِ الدَّالَّةِ عَلَى الذَّاتِ المُتَّصِفِ بِالصِّفَاتِ؛ لِأَنَّ المَقْصُوْدَ فِي اعْتِقَادِ المُكَلَّفِيْنَ اتِّصَافُ اللَّهِ بِالصِّفَاتِ، وَلِوُرُوْدِ الأَسْمَاءِ فِي الكِتَابِ وَالسُّنَّةِ.

The versifier mentioned thirteen attributes by mentioning the names that denote the being which is attributed with the[se] attributes. [This is] because the objective of the beliefs of responsible individuals is to attribute the attributes to Allah; and since the names are mentioned in the Book [the Quran] and the Sunnah.

فالإِسْمُ الأَوَّلُ دَالٌّ عَلَى الصِّفَةِ(33) النَّفسِيَّةِ، وَهِيَ: الوُجُوْدُ.

The first name denotes the essential (or personal) attribute [*al-ṣifat al-nafsiyyah*]. It is Existence.[34]

وَالأَسْمَاءُ الخَمْسَةُ دَالَّةٌ عَلَى الصِّفَاتِ السَّلْبِيَّةِ، وَهِيَ: القِدَمُ، وَالبَقَاءُ، وَالمُخَالَفَةُ لِلخَلْقِ، وَالغِنَاءُ عَنْ الذَّاتِ وَالفاعِلُ، وَالوَحْدَانِيَّةُ.

The [next] five names denote the apophatic attributes [*al-ṣifāt al-salbiyyah*]. They are Beginninglessness, Everlastingness, Dissimilarity to creation, Free of need of entities and actors, and Oneness.[35]

---

32 Ustaz Zainul Abidin mentioned that A has «ثلاثة عشر», and perhaps what is mentioned here is better since it follows Arabic grammar for compound numbering.

33 Ustaz Zainul Abidin mentioned that A has «الصفات», and perhaps what is mentioned here is better.

34 *Jawharah*, 23; *Tuḥfah*, 140–141.

35 Beginningless: *Jawharah*, 23; *Tuḥfah*, 142. Perpetualness: *Jawharah*, 23; *Tuḥfah*, 143–46. Dissimilarity to creation: *Jawharah*, 24; *Tuḥfah*, 147–48. Free of need:

وَالأَسْـمَاءُ السَّـبْعَةُ دَالَّةٌ عَلَى صِفَاتِ المَعَانِي، وَهِـيَ: الحَيَاةُ، وَالقُدْرَةُ، وَالإِرَادَةُ، وَالعِلْمُ، وَالسَّمْعُ، وَالبَصَرُ، وَالكَلَامُ.

The [next] seven names denote entitative attributes [*ṣifāt al-maʿānī*].[36] They are Living, All-Able, All-Willing, All-Knowing, All-Hearing, All-Seeing, and Speaking.[37]

وَقَوْلُـهُ: «بِذَاتِـهِ»، أَيْ: بِغَيْرِ زَمَانٍ وَلَا نِهَايَةٍ؛ بِمَعْنَى أَنَّهُ تَعَالَى لَا يَسْـبِقُهُ عَدَمٌ وَلَا يَلْحَقُهُ عَدَمٌ، وَهُوَ رَدٌّ لِمَنْ قَالَ: إِنَّهُ تَعَالَى «بَاقٍ بِالبَقَاءِ»، فَجَعَلَ البَقَاءَ مِنْ صِفَاتِ المَعَانِي.

Him [the versifier] saying, "by His essence [*bi-dhātihi*]," i.e. without time or finitude, meaning that He (Most High is He) is not preceded by non-existence, nor followed by non-existence. It rebuts whoever says that He (Most High is He) is perpetual via perpetuity, thus making perpetuity an entitative attribute [i.e. instead of a negative attribute].

وَقَوْلُـهُ: «مُرِيْـدُ كُلِّ شَـيْءٍ»، أَيْ: وَاقِعٍ فِـي العَالَمِ مِنْ خَيْرٍ وَشَـرٍّ وَطَاعَةٍ وَمَعْصِيَةٍ، لَا تَتَحَرَّكُ ذَرَّةٌ إِلَّا بِأَمْرِهِ، وَلَا تَسْقُطُ وَرَقَةٌ إِلَّا بِعِلْمِهِ.

Him saying, "All-Willing of everything," i.e. whatever occurs in the universe, of good and bad, and obedience and disobedience.[38] No speck moves save by His command, and no leaf falls except by His knowledge.

Jawharah, 25; *Tuḥfah*, 149–51. Oneness: *Jawharah*, 25, 26; *Tuḥfah*, 152–154, 157–167.

36 *Jawharah*, 27; *Tuḥfah*, 168.

37 Living: *Jawharah*, 29; *Tuḥfah*, 186–87. All-Able: *Jawharah*, 27; *Tuḥfah*, 169–70. All-Willing: *Jawharah*, 27; *Tuḥfah*, 171–77. All-Knowing: *Jawharah*, 28; *Tuḥfah*, 178–85. All-Hearing: *Jawharah*, 29; *Tuḥfah*, 194–95. All-Seeing: *Jawharah*, 29; *Tuḥfah*, 196–201. Speaking: *Jawharah*, 29; *Tuḥfah*, 189–93.

38 *Jawharah*, 27; *Tuḥfah*, 173–77.

قَوْلُـهُ: «بِلَا شَـبَهٍ عَلَى البَشَـرِ»، أَيْ: أَنَّ كَلَامَهُ تَعَالَـى لَيْسَ بِحَرْفٍ وَلَا صَوْتٍ وَلَا انْتِهَاءٍ، مُنَزَّهَةٌ عَنِ التَّقَدُّمِ وَالتَّأَخُّرِ وَالسُّـكُوْنِ(39) النَّفْسِـيِّ وَعَنْ جَمِيْعِ صِفَاتِ كَلَامِ الحَوَادِثِ.

Him saying, "without resembling human beings," i.e. His speech (Most High is He) is not through phonemes, nor sounds, nor ending. It [i.e. His speech] is free from temporal sequence and the cessation of self-thought,[40] and from all the attributes of the speech of contingent [i.e. created] beings.

وَحَيْثُ وَجَبَتْ لَهُ تَعَالَى هَذِهِ الصِّفَاتُ اسْتَحَالَتْ عَلَيْهِ تَعَالَى أَضْدَادُهَا.

Since these attributes are necessary for Him (Most High is He), their opposites are impossible for Him (Most High is He).

(٧) كُـلُّ كَـمَـالٍ وَاجِـبٌ لِـذَاتِـهِ * وَكُـلُّ نَقْصٍ مُمْتَنِعْ فِي حَقِّهِ

(7) Every perfection is necessary for His essence * Every deficiency is impossible for Him

أَيْ: يَجِبُ عَلَى كُلِّ مُكَلَّفٍ أَنْ يَعْتَقِدَ إِجْمَالًا أَنَّهُ تَعَالَى مُتَّصِفٌ بِجَمِيْعِ الكَمَالَاتِ الَّتِي لَا يُحْصِيهَا إِلَّا هُوَ، وَأَنَّهُ تَعَالَى مُنَزَّهٌ عَنْ جَمِيْعِ النَّقَائِصِ الَّتِي لَا يُحْصِيهَا إِلَّا هُوَ.

It is obligatory for every responsible individual to believe, in general, that He (Most High is He) is characterised by all perfections, which only He can enumerate; and that He is free of all imperfections, which only He can enumerate.

39 A: «والسكون». TM: «السكوت».
40 *Jawharah*, 29; *Tuḥfah*, 189.

WHAT IS POSSIBLE FOR HIM (GLORIOUS IS HE) [ما يَجوزُ في حَقِّهِ سُبحانَهُ]

(٨) وَفِعْلُ مُمْكِنْ جَائِزٌ فِي حَقِّهِ * كَـرَزْقِـهِ الخَيْرَ وَبَـعْـثِ رُسْـلِـهِ

(8) Performing the possible is permissible for Him * Like His giving good sustenance and sending His messengers

أَي: يَجِـبُ عَلَـى كُلِّ مُكَلَّفٍ أَنْ يَعْتَقِـدَ أَنَّ الجَائِزَ فِي حَقِّهِ تَعَالَى فِعْلُ كُلِّ مُمْكِنٍ.

Meaning: It is obligatory for every responsible individual to believe that it is permissible for Him (Most High is He) to perform anything that is [rationally] possible.[41]

قَوْلُـهُ: «كَرَزْقِـهِ» بِفَتْحِ الرَّاءِ، هُـوَ مِنْ إِضَافَةِ المَصْـدَرِ لِفَاعِلِهِ، وَالمَفْعُوْلُ الأَوَّلُ مَحْـذُوْفٌ، وَ«الخَيْـرَ» مَفْعُوْلُـهُ الثَّانِي. وَالتَّقْدِيْرُ: كَـرَزْقِ اللّٰهِ العَبْدَ الخَيْرَ.

Him saying, "like giving sustenance [*razqihi*]" (with a *fatḥah* on the *rā'*) is out of relating the verbal noun [i.e. *razq-*] to its actor [i.e. *-hi*], with the first object [i.e. *al-'abd* ("the slave")] being elided and "good [*al-khayr*]" being its second object. Its syntactic interpolation is: "Like Allah (Most High is He) giving servants good sustenance."

والأَرْزَاقُ نَوْعَـانِ: ظَاهِـرَةٌ لِلأَبْـدَانِ كَالأَقْـوَاتِ، وَباطِنَـةٌ لِلقُلُـوْبِ كَالعُلُوْمِ وَالمَعَارِفِ.

Sustenance is two types: external, which is for bodies (like staple

41 *Jawharah*, 44; *Tuḥfah*, 285.

foods); and internal, which is for hearts (like knowledge and experiences).[42]

وَيَجِبُ أَنْ يَعْتَقِدَ أَنَّ مِنَ الجَائِزِ فِي حَقِّهِ تَعَالَى إِرْسَالُ الرُّسُلِ مِنْ آدَمٍ إِلَى مُحَمَّدٍ ﷺ وَعَلَيْهِمْ أَجْمَعِيْنَ.

It is obligatory to believe that among what is permissible for Him (Most High is He) is sending the Messengers,[43] from Ādam to Muḥammad (may Allah bless him and give him peace, and upon all of them).

42 *Jawharah*, 100; *Tuḥfah*, 735.

43 *Jawharah*, 57–58; *Tuḥfah*, 391–402.

2

MATTERS RELATED TO THE PROPHETS

[قِسمُ النُّبُوِّيَاتِ]

ثُمَّ شَرَعَ النَّاظِمُ فِي القِسْمِ الثَّانِي، وَهُوَ النُّبُوِّيَّاتُ، فَقَالَ:

The versifier then began the second section, which is matters related to the prophets [*al-nubuwwiyyāt*]. He said:

WHAT IS NECESSARY FOR THE NOBLE MESSENGERS ﷺ

[ما يَجِبُ في حَقِّ الرُّسُلِ الكِرام ﷺ]

(٩) وَوَاجِبٌ لَهُمْ بَلَاغٌ صِدْقُ * وَعِصْمَةٌ مِمَّا نُهِيْ وَحِذْقُ

(9) Necessary for them are conveying, truthfulness, * Preservation from committing what is forbidden and intelligence

أَي: يَجِبُ عَلَيْهِ أَنْ يَعْتَقِدَ أَنَّ الوَاجِبَ فِي حَقِّ الرُّسُلِ أَرْبَعَةٌ.

Meaning: It is obligatory for him [i.e. a responsible individual] to believe that four [things] are necessary for the messengers.

الأَوَّلُ: تَبْلِيْغُهُمْ لِجَمِيْعِ مَا أُمِرُوْا بِتَبْلِيْغِهِ لِلخَلْقِ بِخِلَافِ مَا أُمِرُوْا بِكِتْمَانِهِ وَمَا خُيِّرُوْا فِيْهِ.

The first is their reporting everything they were commanded to convey to creation—in contrast to what they were commanded to conceal and what they were given a choice for [whether or not to convey].[44]

الثَّانِي: الصِّدْقُ، وَهُوَ مُطَابَقَةُ خَبَرِهِمْ لِلْوَاقِعِ وَلَوْ بِحَسَبِ اعْتِقَادِهِمْ.

The second is truthfulness, which is their statements matching reality—even if [that match is] according to their beliefs [and not things as they truly are].[45]

وَالثَّالِثُ: العِصْمَةُ، وَهِيَ حِفْظُ ظَوَاهِرِهِمْ وَبَوَاطِنِهِمْ مِنَ التَّلَبُّسِ بِمَنْهِيٍّ عَنْهُ وَلَوْ نَهْيَ كَرَاهَةٍ أَوْ خِلَافَ الأَوْلَى. فَهُمْ مَعْصُومُونَ عَنْ جَمِيعِ المَعَاصِي المُتَعَلِّقَةِ بِظَاهِرِ البَدَنِ كَالزِّنَا وَشُرْبِ الخَمْرِ وَغَيْرِ ذَلِكَ، وَعَنْ جَمِيعِ المُتَعَلِّقَةِ بِالبَاطِنِ مِنَ الحَسَدِ وَالكِبْرِ وَالرِّيَاءِ وَغَيْرِ ذَلِكَ.

The third is their preservation, which is protecting their bodies and minds[46] from engaging in anything forbidden—even something forbidden for being offensive or even suboptimal. They are protected from all disobedience that is associated with the exetrnal of the body (including fornication, drinking wine, and others) and from all that is associated with its internal (including envy, arrogance, showing off, and others).[47]

---

44 *Jawharah*, 60; *Tuḥfah*, 412–14.

45 *Jawharah*, 59; *Tuḥfah*, 408–9, which mentions that this is such as him ﷺ saying, "None of that happened," when Dhu-l-Yadayn asked, "Did the prayer shorten, or did you forget, O Messenger of Allah?," when he ﷺ gave the prayer's closing *taslīm* after two *rak'ats*. The hadith is mentioned in al-Bukhārī, 1229; Muslim, 573.

46 The Arabic uses the words *ẓawāhir* and *bawāṭin*, which each has a range of meanings, including external and visible, and inward and hidden (respectively). In the given context, the former can refer to the protection of the body and its acts, and the latter to the protection of the spirit, mind, morality, and character.

47 *Jawharah*, 29, 68; *Tuḥfah*, 200–201, 465.

والرّابِعُ: الحِذْقُ، وَهُوَ المَهَارَةُ فِي الأُمُورِ وَالتَّفَطُّنُ وَالتَّيَقُّظُ لِإِلْزَامِ الخُصُومِ وَإِبْطَالِ دَعَاوِيْهِمْ البَاطِلَةِ.

The fourth is intelligence, which is having expertise in matters, astuteness, and alertness. [All are] in order to force opponents to accept an argument, and to invalidate their false claims.[48]

WHAT IS IMPOSSIBLE AND PERMISSIBLE FOR THEM ﷩ [ما يَستَحيلُ في حَقِّهِم ﷩ وَما يَجوزُ]

(١٠) وَضِدَّهَا نَزِّهْ كَكُلِّ قَادِحْ * وَغَيْرُهُ يَجُوزُ مِنْ أَكْلٍ نِكَاحْ

(10) Declare [them] free from their opposites (like all that impugns). * And others are permissible (including eating and marriage)

أَي: يَسْتَحِيْلُ فِي حَقِّهِمْ -عَلَيْهِمُ الصَّلَاةُ وَالسَّلَامُ- أَضْدَادُ تِلْكَ الأَرْبَعَةِ.

Meaning: The opposites of the four are impossible for them (may Allah bless them and give them peace).[49]

وَهُوَ: كِتْمَانُ شَيْءٍ مِمَّا أُمِرُوْا بِتَبْلِيْغِهِ، وَالكَذِبُ، وَالخِيَانَةُ بِفِعْلِ شَيْءٍ مِمَّا نُهِيَ عَنْهُ نَهْيَ تَحْرِيْمٍ أَوْ كَرَاهَةٍ؛ فَلَا يَقَعُ مِنْهُمْ مَكْرُوْهٌ وَلَا خِلَافُ أَوْلَى بَلْ وَلَا مُبَاحٌ، وَإِذَا وَقَعَتْ[50] صُوْرَةُ ذَلِكَ مِنْهُمْ فَهُوَ لِلتَّشْرِيْعِ، فَيَصِيْرُ وَاجِبًا أَوْ مَنْدُوْبًا فِي حَقِّهِمْ؛ فَأَفْعَالُهُمْ دَائِرَةٌ بَيْنَ الوَاجِبِ وَالمَنْدُوْبِ، وَالبَلَادَةُ. ومَعْنَى اسْتِحَالَةِ هَذِهِ الأَرْبَعَةِ عَدَمُ قَبُوْلِهَا الثُّبُوْتَ بِالدَّلِيْلِ الشَّرْعِيِّ.

48 *Jawharah*, 59; *Tuḥfah*, 410–11.

49 *Jawharah*, 60; *Tuḥfah*, 415.

50 Ustaz Zainul Abidin mentioned that A has «وقع», and perhaps what is mentioned here is better.

They are: concealing anything they were commanded to convey; lying; treachery by performing anything that is forbidden—whether unlawful or offensive.

Nothing they perform is offensive or suboptimal—nor merely permissible [*mubāḥ*]. When something in the form of a forbidden act does occur from them, it is for the sake of legislation and thus, for them, obligatory or recommended. Therefore, their actions waver between obligatory and recommended.

[The fourth of the opposites that are impossible for them is] stupidity.

What is meant by the impossibility of these four things is that they [the acts] do not accept coming into existence, as attested by legislative evidence.[51]

وَيَجُوزُ فِي حَقِّهِمْ -عَلَيْهِمْ الصَّلَاةُ وَالسَّلَامُ- كُلُّ مَا هُوَ مِنْ الأَعْرَاضِ البَشَرِيَّةِ الَّتِي لَا تُؤَدِّي إِلَى نَقْصٍ فِي مَرَاتِبِهِمْ العَلِيَّةِ كَالأَكْلِ وَالشُّرْبِ وَالنَّوْمِ وَالبَيْعِ وَالشِّرَاءِ وَالمَشِي وَالرُّكُوْبِ.

All the various human conditions which do not detract from their high station are possible for them (may Allah bless them and give them peace), such as eating, drinking, sleeping, buying, selling, walking, and riding.[52]

وَقَوْلُهُ: «نِكَاحٍ»، المُرَادُ بِهِ هُنا جِمَاعٌ لِلنِّسَاءِ عَلَى وَجْهِ الحِلِّ.

Him [the versifier] saying, "like marriage": what is intended here is intercourse with women in a licit manner.[53]

51 *Jawharah*, 60; *Tuḥfah*, 416.
52 *Jawharah*, 61; *Tuḥfah*, 417–18, 422.
53 *Jawharah*, 61; *Tuḥfah*, 419–21.

وَمِنْ الجَائِزِ فِي حَقِّهِمْ المَرَضُ غَيْرُ المُنَفِّرِ.

Among the things that are possible for them is non-repulsive sickness.

3

MATTERS KNOWN THROUGH REVELATION

[قِسمُ السَّمْعِيَّاتِ]

ثُمَّ شَرَعَ النَّاظِمُ فِي القِسْمِ الثَّالِثِ وَهُوَ السَّمْعِيَّاتِ، فَقَالَ:

The versifier then began the third section, which is revealed matters [*al-sam'iyyāt*]. He said:

PROPHETS, MESSENGERS, BOOKS, ANGELIC SCRIBES

[الإيمانُ بِالأَنبياءِ وَالرُّسُلِ وَالكُتُبِ وَالكاتِبينَ]

(١١) وَوَاجِبٌ إِيْمَانُنَا بِالمُرْسَلِيْنْ * وَالأَنْبِيَا وَكُتُبٍ وَالكَاتِبِيْنْ

(11) Our belief in the messengers is obligatory * And the prophets, books, and the [angelic] scribes

أَي: يَجِبُ عَلَى كُلِّ مُكَلَّفٍ أَنْ يُصَدِّقَ بِأَنَّ لِلَّهِ رُسُلًا وَأَنْبِيَاءٍ عَلَى الإِجْمَالِ.

Meaning: It is obligatory for every responsible individual to believe, in general, that Allah sent messengers and prophets.

وَالمَشْهُوْرُ أَنَّ المُرْسَلِيْنَ ثَلَاثُمِائَةٍ وَثَلَاثَةَ عَشَرَ، وَأَنَّ الأَنْبِيَاءَ غَيْرَ المُرْسَلِيْنَ

مِائَةُ أَلْفٍ وَثَلَاثَةٌ وَعِشْرُوْنَ أَلْفًا وَسِتُّمِائَةٍ وَسَبْعَةٌ وَثَمَانُوْنَ نَبِيًّا. وَهُمْ يَتَفَاضَلُوْنَ فِيْمَا بَيْنَهُمْ عِنْدَ اللّٰهِ.

The well-known opinion is that there were 313 messengers,[54] and 123,687 prophets who were not messengers (i.e. prophets).[55] They vary in their [degree of] excellence with Allah.[56]

وَالأَسْلَمُ الإِمْسَاكُ عَنْ حَصْرِهِمَا فِي عَدَدٍ.

It is safest to refrain from limiting them to a [specific or finite] number.[57]

وَيَجِبُ عَلَيْهِ أَنْ يَعْتَقِدَ أَنَّ اللّٰهَ أَنْزَلَ كُتُبًا مِنَ السَّمَاءِ عَلَى الإِجْمَالِ، وَالتَّحْقِيْقُ الإِمْسَاكُ عَنْ حَصْرِهَا فِي عَدَدٍ.

It is obligatory for him [a responsible individual] to believe that Allah revealed books from the heavens in general. After critical examination, the best opinion is to refrain from limiting them to a [specific or finite] number.

وَيَجِبُ الإِيْمَانُ بِالكِرَامِ الكَاتِبِيْنَ، وَهُوَ ثَلَاثَةُ أَقْسَامٍ: الكَاتِبِيْنَ عَلَى العِبَادِ أَعْمَالَهُمْ فِي الدُّنْيَا، وَالكَاتِبُوْنَ مِنَ اللَّوْحِ المَحْفُوْظِ مَا فِي صُحُفِ

---

54 Al-Ḥākim, *Al-Mustadrak*, 4166; al-Bayhaqī, *Shu'ab al-īmān*, 131.

55 The author mentions this opinion in some of his other works, including *Al-Thimār al-yāni'* (Beirut: Dār al-Kutub al-'Ilmiyyah, 2013/1434), p24. In *Qaṭar al-ghayth*, he gives two hadiths in support of Abū Ghayth al-Samarqandī's saying that their number is 124,000. The hadith is mentioned in Ibn Ḥibbān (361) and others. For more details, see al-Suyūṭī *Jāmi' al-aḥādīth*, 20927.

56 The best of all creation is our Prophet ﷺ, followed by Ibrāhīm, Mūsā, 'Īsā, and Nūḥ. They are followed by the remaining messengers, then the remaining prophets who were not messengers—with variations in their ranks with Allah. (May Allah bless them all and give them peace.) See the author's commentary *Tījān al-darādīr*, printed within *Majmū' shams rasā'il fī l-'aqā'id* (Amman: Dār al-nūr al-mubīn, 2013), 210.

57 *Jawharah*, 58; *Tuḥfah*, 400.

المَلَائِكَةِ المُوَكَّلِيْنَ بِالتَّصَرُّفِ فِي العَالَمِ كُلَّ عَامٍ، وَالكَاتِبُوْنَ مِنْ صُحُفِ المَلَائِكَةِ كِتابًا يُوضَعُ تَحْتَ العَرْشِ.

It is obligatory to believe in the noble recorders. They are three divisions:

1 Those who record a servant's actions in this life.
2 Those who, every year, transcribe from the Protected Tablet into the scrolls of angels charged with discharging things in the world.
3 Those who transcribe from the scrolls of the angels into a single book that is placed below the throne.[58]

وَكُلُّ ذَلِكَ أَوْجَدَهُ اللّٰهُ لِحُكْمٍ يَعْلَمُهَا اللّٰهُ تَعَالَى.

Allah has brought all of these into existence for a wisdom known to Allah (Most High is He).

THE RESURRECTION, WATERING POOL, ACCOUNTING [الإيمانُ بِالبَعثِ وَالحَوضِ وَالحِسابِ]

(١٢) وَالبَعْثِ وَالحَوْضِ وَبِالحِسَابِ * وَالـوَزْنِ وَالـصِّـرَاطِ وَالـكِـتَـابِ

(12) And [in] the resurrection, the watering pool, and accounting * And the scale, the bridge, and the book

أَي: يَجِبُ الإِيْمَانُ بِالبَعْثِ لِلحَشْرِ.

Meaning: It is obligatory to believe in the resurrection for being gathered.

58 *Jawharah*, 107; *Tuḥfah*, 682.

فالبَعْثُ إِحْيَاءُ المَوْتَى وَإِخْرَاجُهُمْ مِنْ قُبُوْرِهِمْ بِأَنْ يُوْجِدُ اللَّهُ الأَجْسَامَ بَعْدَ العَدَمِ المَحْضِ بِجَمِيْعِ أَجْزَائِهَا الأَصْلِيَّةِ؛ أَي: الَّتِي مِنْ شَأْنِهَا البَقَاءُ مِنْ أَوَّلِ العُمْرِ إِلَى آخِرِهِ وَلَوْ قُطِعَتْ قَبْلَ المَوْتِ.

The resurrection is the dead being brought to life and their being removed from their graves. [It happens] by Allah bringing the bodies into existence after their complete non-existence with all of their original parts (i.e. those which have the nature of remaining from the beginning of life until its end)—even if it was severed before death.[59]

وَالحَشْرُ عِبَارَةٌ عَنْ سَوْقِهِمْ جَمِيْعًا إِلَى المَوْقِفِ، وَلَا فَرْقَ بَيْنَ مَنْ يُجَازَى -وَهُمْ الإِنْسُ وَالجِنُّ وَالمَلَكُ- وَبَيْنَ مَنْ لَا يُجَازَى - وَهُمْ الوُحُوْشِ.

The gathering refers to driving them all together [i.e. the resurrected] to where they will stand waiting [for judgment, *al-mawqif*]. There is no difference between those who will be recompensed (humans, jinn, and angels) and those who will not (beasts).[60]

وَيَجِبُ الإِيْمَانُ بِحَوْضِهِ ﷺ، وَيُفَسَّقُ مَنْ أَنْكَرَهُ وَلَا يُكَفَّرُ. وَقَدْ وُرِدَتْ أَنَّ لِكُلِّ نَبِيٍّ حَوْضًا تَرِدُهُ أُمَّتُهُ.

It is obligatory to believe in his watering pool ﷺ.[61] Whoever denies it is considered corrupt but is not considered a disbeliever. It has been transmitted that every prophet has a watering pool that his community will pass by.[62]

وَبِالحِسَـابِ، وَهُوَ تَوْقِيْفُ النَّاسِ عَلَى أَعْمَالِهِمْ خَيْرًا كَانَتْ أَوْ شَـرًّا، قَوْلًا

59 *Jawharah*, 96; *Tuḥfah*, 619.
60 *Jawharah*, 96; *Tuḥfah*, 620.
61 *Jawharah*, 95; *Tuḥfah*, 699.
62 *Jawharah*, 95; *Tuḥfah*, 700.

كَانَتْ أَوْ فِعْلًا، تَفْصِيْلًا، بَعْدَ أَخْذِهِمْ كُتُبَهَا، وَيَكُوْنَ لِلْمُؤْمِنِ وَالكَافِرِ إِنْسًا وَجِنًّا إِلَّا مَنْ اسْتُثْنِيَ مِنْ مُؤْمِنِي هَذِهِ الأُمَّةِ. وَقَدْ وُرِدَ أَنَّ الكُفَّارَ يُنْكِرُوْنَ، فَتَشْهَدُ عَلَيْهِمْ أَلْسِنَتُهُمْ وَأَيْدِيْهِمْ وَأَرْجُلُهُمْ وَأَسْمَاعُهُمْ وَأَبْصَارُهُمْ وَجُلُوْدُهُمْ وَالأَرْضُ وَاللَّيْلُ وَالنَّهَارُ وَالحَفَظَةُ الكِرَامُ.

[It is obligatory to believe] in the accounting, which is people being apprised of their actions (good and bad, words and deeds), in detail, after they take their books.[63] It will happen for believers and disbelievers (humans and jinn), except the believers of this community who have been exempted.[64] It has been transmitted that the disbelievers will reject it,[65] so their tongues, hands, legs,[66] hearing, vision, skin,[67] the ground, the night, the day, and the noble recording angels will testify against them.[68]

THE SCALE, BRIDGE, BOOK OF DEEDS [الإيمانُ بِالوَزنِ وَالصِّراطِ وَالكِتابِ]

ثُمَّ بَعْدَ الحِسَابِ يُؤْمَرُ بِالنَّاسِ إِلَى المِيْزَانِ. قَالَ تَعَالَى: ﴿وَالْوَزْنُ يَوْمَئِذٍ الْحَقُّ﴾. وَلَا يَكُوْنُ الوَزْنُ فِي حَقِّ الأَنْبِيَاءِ وَالمَلَائِكَةِ وَمَنْ يَدْخُلُ الجَنَّةَ بِغَيْرِ حِسَابٍ؛ لِأَنَّهُ فَرْعٌ عَنِ الحِسَابِ.

Then, after the accounting, people will be commanded to go to the scales.[69] Allah (Most High is He) says, "And the weighing [of deeds]

63 *Jawharah*, 100; *Tuḥfah*, 637.
64 Muslim, 546.
65 *Jawharah*, 100; *Tuḥfah*, 637–638.
66 Nur, 24:24.
67 Fuṣṣilat, 41:19–24.
68 Muslim, 2969; cf Qāf, 50:21–23.
69 *Jawharah*, 105; *Tuḥfah*, 670.

that Day will be just."[70] The weighing will not happen for prophets, angels, and those who will enter Paradise without accounting since it [weighing] is secondary to the accounting.

وَفِـي وَزْنِ أَعْمَـالِ الكُفَّارِ خِلَافٌ. وَالأَصَحُّ تُوْزَنُ لِأَنَّـهُ يَكُوْنُ مِنْهُمْ صِلَةُ الرَّحِـمِ وَمُوَاسَـاةُ النَّـاسِ وَعِتْـقُ المَمَالِيْـكِ وَنَحْوِهَا مِنَ الأَعْمَـالِ الَّتِي لَا تَتَوَقَّـفُ صِحَّتُهَـا عَلَـى نِيَّـةٍ. فَتُجْعَلُ هَـذِهِ الأُمُوْرِ إِنْ صَـدَرَتْ مِنْهُمْ فِي مُقَابَلَةِ سَيِّآتِهِمْ غَيْرَ الكُفْرِ. أَمَّا هُوَ فَلَا فَائِدَةَ فِي وَزْنِهِ؛ لِأَنَّ عَذَابَهُ دَائِمٌ.

There is disagreement concerning weighing the deeds of disbelievers. The soundest opinion is that they are weighed. [This is] since [their deeds] include maintaining blood ties, assisting others, emancipating slaves, and such deeds that do not depend upon intention for their validity. These deeds, if they performed them, are placed opposite their bad deeds—except for disbelief. As for it [disbelief], there is no benefit in weighing it since its punishment is eternal.[71]

ثُمَّ يَمُرُّ جَمِيْعُ النَّاسِ عَلَى الصِّرَاطِ، لَكِنَّ الكُفَّارَ لَا يَمُرُّوْنَ عَلَى جَمِيْعِهِ، بَـلْ عَلَـى بَعْضِهِ. ثُمَّ يَتَسَـاقَطُوْنَ فِي النَّارِ. وَكُلُّهُمْ سَـاكِتُوْنَ إِلَّا الأَنْبِيَاءُ، فَيَقُوْلُوْنَ: «اللَّهُمَّ سَـلِّمْ سَـلِّمْ!»، وَسَيِّدُنَا مُحَمَّدٌ ﷺ يَقُوْلُ: «أُمَّتِي أُمَّتِي! لَا أَسْـأَلُكَ [اليَوْمَ(72)] نَفْسِـي وَلَا فَاطِمَةَ بِنْتِي»، وَهُوَ جِسْرٌ مَمْدُوْدٌ عَلَى مَتْنِ جَهَنَّمَ، أَوَّلُهُ فِي المَوْقِفِ وَآخِرُهُ إِلَى الجَنَّةِ.

Then, all people will pass over the *ṣirāt* [the bridge that extends over Hell].[73] However, the disbelievers will not pass over its entirety. Rather, [they will pass over] part of it and then fall into the fire. Everyone will be silent except the prophets who will say, "O Allah,

70 Al-Aʿrāf, 7:8.
71 *Jawharah*, 105; *Tuḥfah*, 671.
72 Both sources for the hadith mention «اليوم».
73 *Jawharah*, 106; *Tuḥfah*, 674.

safety! Safety!"[74] And our master Muḥammad ﷺ will say, "[I beg You for] my community! My community![75] I do not beg [You today] for myself or Fāṭimah my daughter!"[76]

It [the *sirāṭ*] is a bridge extending over the body of the hellfire. It begins where judgment is awaited and ends at Paradise.

وَيَجِـبُ الإِيْمَانُ بِثُبُـوْتِ الكِتَابِ المُثْبَتِ فِيْهِ طَاعَـاتُ العِبَادِ وَمَعَاصِيْهِمْ الَّتِي كَتَبَتْهَا المَلَائِكَةُ فِي الدُّنْيَا.

It is obligatory to believe in the existence of the book which contains affirmation of [each] servant's deeds of obedience and disobedience, which the angels recorded in this worldly life.[77]

وَذَلِـكَ تَأْتِـي رِيْحٌ فَتُطِيْرُ كُتُـبَ الأَعْمَالِ مِنْ خِزَانَةٍ تَحْـتَ العَرْشِ فَتَعَلَّقَ كُلُّ صَحِيْفَةٍ بِعُنُقِ صَاحِبِهَا، ثُمَّ تَأْخُذُهَا المَلَائِكَةُ مِنْ أَعْنَاقِهِمْ وَيُنَاوِلُوْنَهَا لَهُـمْ فِي أَيْدِيْهِـمْ. فَالمُؤْمِنُ المُطِيْعُ يَأْخُذُ كِتَابَهُ بِيَمِيْنِـهِ، وَالكَافِرُ يَأْخُذُهُ بِشِمَالِهِ مِنْ وَرَاءِ ظَهْرِهِ.

A wind will blow the books of deeds from a chest beneath the throne,[78] and each scroll will cling to its owner's neck. The angels will then take them [i.e. the scrolls] from their necks and place them in their hands.[79] The obedient believer will take his book in his right hand, and the disbeliever will take his in his left behind his back.[80]

---

74 Al-Bukhārī, 814. cf Jalāl al-Dīn al-Suyūṭī, *Jam' al-jawāmi'*, 24030/75; al-Suyūṭī, *Al-Jāmi' al-ṣaghīr*, 12987, 12989. It is considered sound.

75 Jalāl al-Dīn al-Suyūṭī, *Jam' al-jawāmi'*, 8498/4009, 28402/1775; cf al-Suyūṭī, *Al-Jāmi' al-ṣaghīr*, 2346. It is considered sound.

76 al-Qurṭubī, Al-Tadhkirah bi aḥwāl al-mawt (Riyāḍ: Dār al-Minhāj, 1425), 757.

77 *Jawharah*, 104; *Tuḥfah*, 665–66.

78 Abū Ja'far al-'Uqaylī, *Al-Ḍu'afā' al-kabīr* (Beirut: Dār al-Kutub al-'Ilmiyyah, 1984/1404), 4:466.

79 *Jawharah*, 104; *Tuḥfah*, 667.

80 *Jawharah*, 104; *Tuḥfah*, 667.

THE THRONE, THE STOOL, INTERCESSION

[الإيمانُ بِالعَرْشِ وَالكُرسيِّ وَالشَّفاعَةِ]

(١٣) وَالعَـرْشِ وَالكُرْسِيِّ وَالشَّفَاعَةْ * لَـوْحٍ قَلَـمْ وَبَـرْزَخٍ نَعِيْمَـهْ

(13) And the throne, and the stool, and the intercession, * Tablet, pen, *barzakh,* blissfulness

أي: وَيَجِبُ الإِيْمَانُ بِالعَرْشِ، وَهُوَ جِسْـمٌ عَظِيْمٌ نُوْرَانِيٌّ عُلْوِيٌّ. وَهُوَ قُبَّةٌ فَـوْقَ العَالَـمِ ذَاتُ أَعْمِدَةٍ أَرْبَعَةٍ. تَحْمِلُهُ المَلَائِكَـةُ فِي الدُّنْيَا أَرْبَعَةٌ، وَفِي الآخِرَةِ ثَمَانٌ، رُؤُوْسُـهُمْ عِنْدَ العَرْشِ فِي السَّـمَاءِ السَّـابِعَةِ وَأَقْدَامُهُمْ فِي الأَرْضِ السُّـفْلَى، وَقُرُوْنُهُـمْ كَقُـرُوْنِ الوَعْلِ -أَي: البَقَرُ الوَحْشِـيُّ- مَا بَيْنَ أَصْلِ قَرْنِ أَحَدِهِمْ إِلَى مُنْتَهَاهُ خَمْسُمِائَةُ عَامٍ.

Meaning: It is obligatory to believe in the throne, which is a lofty, enormous luminary body. It is a dome above the universe possessing four pillars carried by the angels: four in this world and eight in the afterworld. Their heads are positioned at the throne in the seventh heaven, and their feet are in the lowest earth. Their horns are like a wild mountain goat (i.e. a wild bull), and between the base and ends of their horns is [a journey lasting] five hundred years.[81]

وَبِالكُرْسِـيِّ، وَهُـوَ جِسْمٌ عَظِيْـمٌ نُوْرَانِـيٌّ تَحْتَ العَـرْشِ مُلْتَصِـقٌ بِهِ فَوْقَ السَّمَاءِ السَّابِعَةِ، بَيْنَهُ وَبَيْنَهَا مَسِيْرَةُ خَمْسُمِائَةُ عَامٍ.

[It is obligatory to believe] in the footstool, which is an enormous luminary body beneath the throne adjacent to it. [It is located] above the seven heavens; between it and them is [a journey lasting] five hundred years.[82]

---

81 *Jawharah*, 107; *Tuḥfah*, 679.
82 *Jawharah*, 107; *Tuḥfah*, 680.

وَيَجِبُ الإِيْمَانُ بِكَوْنِهِ ﷺ شَافِعًا، وَكَوْنِهِ مَقْبُوْلَ الشَّفَاعَةِ، وَكَوْنِهِ مُقَدَّمًا عَلَى غَيْرِهِ. ثُمَّ يَشْفَعُ مَنْ ارْتَضَاهُ اللَّهُ تَعَالَى فِي أَرْبَابِ الكَبَائِرِ، فَيَشْفَعُ كُلٌّ مِنَ الأَنْبِيَاءِ وَالمُرْسَلِيْنَ وَالمَلَائِكَةُ وَالصَّحَابَةِ وَالشُّهَدَاءِ وَالعُلَمَاءِ العَامِلِيْنَ وَالأَوْلِيَاءِ عَلَى قَدْرِ مَقامِهِ عِنْدَ اللَّهِ تَعَالَى.

It is obligatory to believe that he ﷺ is an intercessor,[83] that his intercession is accepted,[84] and that he will intercede before everyone else[85] (followed by whomever Allah wills) concerning those who committed enormities [*kabā'ir*].[86] Thus, all of the prophets, messengers, angels, Companions, martyrs, scholars, and *awliyā'* will intercede to the degree of their station with Allah (Most High is He).

THE TABLET, PEN, *BARZAKH* [الإيمان باللوح والقلم والبرزخ]

وَيَجِبُ الإِيْمَانُ بِاللَّوْحِ، وَهُوَ جِسْمٌ عَظِيْمٌ نُوْرَانِيٌّ، كَتَبَ فِيْهِ القَلَمُ بِإِذْنِ اللَّهِ تَعَالَى مَا كَانَ وَمَا يَكُوْنُ إِلَى يَوْمِ القِيَامَةِ. وبِالقَلَمِ، وَهُوَ جِسْمٌ عَظِيْمٌ نُوْرَانِيٌّ خَلَقَهُ اللهُ تَعَالَى وَأَمَرَهُ بِكَتْبِ مَا كَانَ وَمَا يَكُوْنُ إِلَى يَوْمِ القِيَامَةِ.

It is obligatory to believe in the tablet, which is an enormous luminary body.[87] The pen writes in it by the permission of Allah (Most High is He) what has been and what will be until the Day of Judgment [*yaum al-qiyāmah*].[88]

[It is obligatory to believe] in the pen, which is an enormous luminary body. Allah (Most High is He) created it and ordered it to

83 *Jawharah*, 113–15; *Tuḥfah*, 709–14.
84 *Jawharah*, 113; *Tuḥfah*, 709.
85 *Jawharah*, 113; *Tuḥfah*, 712.
86 *Jawharah*, 116; *Tuḥfah*, 715.
87 *Jawharah*, 107; *Tuḥfah*, 683.
88 *Jawharah*, 107; *Tuḥfah*, 681.

write what has been and what will be until the Day of Judgment [*yaum al-qiyāmah*].

وَيَجِبُ الإِيْمَانُ بِالبَرْزَخِ، وَهُوَ مَا بَيْنَ الدُّنْيَا وَالآخِرَةِ، مِنْ وَقْتِ المَوْتِ إِلَى
البَعْثِ؛ فَمَنْ مَاتَ فَقَدْ دَخَلَ فِي البَرْزَخِ.

It is obligatory to believe in the *barzakh,* which is [a period of time and space] between this world and the afterlife, from the time of death until resurrection. Whoever has died has entered into the *barzakh.*

وَيَجِبُ الإِيْمَانُ بِنَعِيْمِ البَرْزَخِ لِلمُؤْمِنِيْنَ؛ فَلَا يَخْتَصُّ بِهَذِهِ الأُمَّةِ وَلَا
بِالمُكَلَّفِيْنَ. وَمِنْ نَعِيْمِهِ تَوْسِيْعُهُ سَبعِيْنَ ذِرَاعًا عَرْضًا وَكَذَا طُوْلًا. وَمِنْهُ
أَيْضًا فَتْحُ طَاقَةٍ فِيْهِ مِنَ الجَنَّةِ، وَامْتِلَاؤُهُ بِالرَّيْحَانِ، وَجَعْلُهُ رَوْضَةً مِنْ
رِيَاضِ الجَنَّةِ، وَجَعْلُ قَنَدِيْلَ يُنَوِّرُ كَالقَمَرِ لَيْلَةَ البَدْرِ.

It is obligatory to believe in the blissfulness of the *barzakh* for believers.[89] It [this blissfulness] is not limited to this community [i.e. Muslims] nor to legally responsible individuals. Its forms of blissfulness include the grave expanding seventy *dhirā'* in width and also in length[90]. Also from its forms is the opening of an aperture from paradise within it, it being filled with the fragrance [of paradise], it being one of the meadows of paradise, and it being a beacon that shines like the moon on a night with a full moon.[91]

---

89 *Jawharah*, 96; *Tuḥfah*, 615–16.

90 A single *dhirā'* equals approximately 48 centimetres or 18.9 inches, so 70 would equal approximately 33.6 metres or 36.75 yards.

91 The *'ulamā'* understand these to be literal. See *Jawharah*, 96; *Tuḥfah*, 617.

PARADISE AND HELLFIRE [الإيمانُ بِالجَنَّةِ وَالنّارِ]

(١٤) عَــذَابِــهِ وَجَــنَّــةٍ نِــيْــرَانِ * وَالْـحُـوْرِ وَالْـقُـصُـوْرِ وَالْـوِلْـدَانِ

(14) Its torment, and paradise, fire * The houris, the palaces, and the youths

أي: وَيَجِبُ عَلَى المُكَلَّفِ الإِيْمَانُ بِعَذَابِ البَرْزَخِ لِلكَافِرِ وَالمُنَافِقِ وَعُصَاةِ المُؤْمِنِيْــنَ، وَيَــدُوْمُ عَلَى الأَوَّلَيْنِ وَيَنْقَطِعُ عَنْ بَعْضِ عُصَاةِ المُؤْمِنِيْنَ؛ وَهُمْ مَنْ خَفَّتْ جَرَائِمُهُمْ مِنْ العُصَاةِ، فَإِنَّهُمْ يُعَذَّبُوْنَ بِحَسَبِهَا -إِنْ لَمْ يَدْخُلُوْا سَاحَةَ العَفْوِ(92)- وَقَدْ يَرْتَفِعُ عَنْهُمْ بِدُعَاءٍ أَوْ صَدَقَةٍ أَوْ نَحْوِ ذَلِكَ.

It is obligatory for the responsible individual to believe in the torment of the *barzakh* for disbelievers, hypocrites, and disobedient believers. It [the torment] will endure for the first two. It will end for some disobedient believers whose crimes were light, for they will be punished according to their crimes if they did not receive a pardon, and it [i.e. their torture] can be removed through supplication, charity, and the like.[93]

وكُلُّ مَنْ لَا يُسْأَلُ فِي قَبْرِهِ لَا يُعَذَّبُ فِيْهِ.

Everyone who is not interrogated in his grave will not be tortured in it.[94]

والمُعَذَّبُ البَدَنُ وَالرُّوْحُ جَمِيْعًا بِاتِّفَاقِ أَهْلِ الحَقِّ. وَيَخْلُقُ اللهُ فِيْهِ إِدْرَاكًا بِحَيْثُ يَعْلَمُ وَيَسْمَعُ وَيَتَلَذَّذُ وَيَتَأَلَّمُ.

---

92 *Tuḥfah* lacks this sentence.

93 *Jawharah*, 96; *Tuḥfah*, 613.

94 *Jawharah*, 96; *Tuḥfah*, 613.

What is tormented is the body and the spirit together, by agreement of *Ahl al-Ḥaqq*. Within it [i.e. *barzakh*], Allah makes one aware such that one knows, hears, feels pleasure, and feels pain.[95]

وَيَجِبُ الإِيْمَانُ بِالجَنَّةِ؛ وَهِيَ دارُ الثَّوَابِ، وَبِالنِّيْرَانِ؛ وَهِيَ دارُ العَذَابِ،
وَبِكَوْنِهِمَا مَوْجُوْدَتَيْنِ(96) فِيْمَا مَضَى.

It is obligatory to believe in paradise (the abode of reward) and hellfire (the abode of torture) and that they both have existed in the past.[97]

فَالنَّاسُ يَكُوْنُوْنَ فِي المَوْقِفِ عَلَى حَالَتِهِمْ الَّتِي مَاتُوْا عَلَيْهَا وَيَكُوْنُوْنَ غُرْلًا
وَتَكُوْنُ هَذِهِ الأُمَّةُ غُرًّا مُحَجَّلِيْنَ.

In the place of standing [for judgment, *al-mawqif*], people will be in the [same] condition as when they died, and they will be uncircumcised.[98] This community [i.e. Muslims] will have white faces and limbs [bright from making ablution].[99]

ثُمَّ يَدْخُلُ المُؤْمِنُوْنَ الجَنَّةَ جُرْدًا مُرْدًا أَبْنَاءَ ثَلَاثٍ وَثَلَاثِيْنَ سَنَةً، طُوْلُ كُلِّ
وَاحِدٍ مِنْهُمْ سِتُّوْنَ ذِراعًا، وَعَرْضُهُ سَبْعَةَ أَذْرُعٍ، ثُمَّ لَا يَزِيْدُوْنَ وَلَا يَنْقُصُوْنَ.

The believers will then enter paradise. [They will be] without body hair or beard hair, thirty-three years of age. Each one will be sixty *dhirā'* tall and seven *dhirā'* wide,[100] and they will not increase or

95 *Jawharah*, 96; *Tuḥfah*, 613.

96 Ustaz Zainul Abidin mentioned that A has «موجودتان», and perhaps what is mentioned here is better.

97 *Jawharah*, 106; *Tuḥfah*, 687.

98 Al-Bukhārī, 6606; Muslim 7377.

99 *Jawharah*, 110; *Tuḥfah*, 698.

100 A single *dhirā'* equals approximately 48 centimetres or 18.9 inches, so 60 would equal approximately 28.8 metres or 31.5 yards, and 7 would equal approximately 3.36 metres or 3.675 yards. *Jawharah*, 110; *Tuḥfah*, 698.

decrease [i.e. in age or size].[101]

أَمَّـا أَجْسَـامُ الكُفَّارِ فِي جَهَنَّـمَ فَمُخْتَلِفَةُ المَقَادِيْرِ، حَتَّـى وُرِدَ أَنَّ ضِرْسَ الكَافِـرِ مِثْـلُ أُحُدٍ، وَفَخِـذُهُ مِثْلُ وَرِقَانَ -وَهُمَا جَبَـلَانِ بِالمَدِيْنَةِ، وَمَا بَيْنَ شَـحْمَتَي أُذُنِ أَحَدِهِـمْ وَعَاتِقِـهِ سَـبْعُوْنَ خَرِيْفًـا تَجْرِي فِيْهَـا أَوْدِيَةُ القَيْحِ وَالدَّمِ، وَغِلَظُ جِلْدِهِ مَسِيْرَةُ ثَلَاثَةِ أَيَّامٍ لِلرَّاكِبِ المُسْرِعِ.

The bodies of disbelievers in hellfire will be of differing proportions. It has even been transmitted that the molars of disbelievers will be like Uḥud and their thighs like Wariqān (which are both mountains in Medina),[102] and between their earlobes and shoulders is [a distance whose traversal requires] seventy autumns,[103] with valleys of puss and blood flowing through it. The thickness of their skin will be the distance a speedy rider travels in three days.[104]

THE HOURIS, PALACES, YOUTHS OF PARADISE [الإيمانُ بِالحورِ العَينِ وَالقُصورِ وَالوِلدانِ]

وَيَجِـبُ الإِيْمَانُ بِالحُـوْرِ العِيْنِ، قَالَ اللَّهُ تَعَالَى: ﴿وَحُوْرٌ عِيْنٌ * كَأَمْثَالِ اللُّؤْلُؤِ الْمَكْنُوْنِ﴾ أَي: فِي صَفَاءِ اللُّؤْلُؤِ مَعَ صُفْرَةٍ فِي بَيَاضِهِنَّ.

It is obligatory to believe in the houris. Allah (Most High is He) says, "And [they will have] maidens with wide, lovely eyes, * the likenesses of untouched pearls,"[105] i.e. the purity of pearls, with a yellow tinge in the whites of their eyes.

---

101 For the height and age not changing, see al-Bukhārī, 3326; Muslim, 2841 #28.

102 Aḥmed, 8345; Al-Tirmidhi, 2578; al-Ḥākim, 8771. *Jawharah*, 110; *Tuḥfah*, 698.

103 al-Bayhaqī, *Al-Bi'th wa al-nushūr* (Beirut: Markaz al-Khidamāt wa-l-Abḥāth, 1986/1406), #573.

104 Muslim, 2851 #44.

105 Al-Wāqi'ah, 56:22–23.

وبِالقُصُورِ، أَي: الغُرَفِ وَالخِيَامِ المُعَدَّةِ لِأَهْلِ الجَنَّةِ، قَالَ اللَّهُ تَعَالَى: ﴿لَٰكِنِ الَّذِينَ اتَّقَوْا رَبَّهُمْ لَهُمْ غُرَفٌ مِّن فَوْقِهَا غُرَفٌ مَّبْنِيَّةٌ تَجْرِي مِن تَحْتِهَا الْأَنْهَارُ﴾.

[It is obligatory to believe] in the palaces (i.e. the rooms and tents) prepared for the people of paradise. Allah (Most High is He) says, "But those who keep their duty to their Lord, for them are lofty halls built above the other, beneath which rivers flow."[106]

وَقَالَ ﷺ: «دَخَلْتُ الجَنَّةَ فَإِذَا أَنَا بِقَصْرٍ مِنْ ذَهَبٍ فَقُلْتُ: لِمَنْ هَذَا؟، فَقَالُوا: لِشَابٍّ مِنْ قُرَيْشٍ، فَظَنَنْتُ أَنِّي(107) أَنَا هُوَ، فَقُلْتُ: وَمَنْ هُوَ؟، قَالُوا: لِعُمَرَ بْنِ الخَطَّابِ».

He ﷺ said, "I entered paradise and, behold, I was at a palace made of gold. I asked, 'Whose is this?' They said, 'A youth from Quraish.' I thought it was me, so I asked, 'Who is he?' They said, 'It belongs to 'Umar bin al-Khaṭṭāb.'"[108]

وَقَالَ ﷺ: «فِي الْجَنَّةِ خَيْمَةٌ مِنْ لُؤْلُؤَةٍ مُجَوَّفَةٍ عَرْضُهَا سِتُّونَ(109) مِيْلًا فِي كُلِّ زَاوِيَةٍ مِنْهَا أَهْلٌ لِلمُؤْمِنِينَ(110) مَا يَرَوْنَ الآخَرِينَ، يَطُوفُ عَلَيْهِمُ المُؤْمِنُ».

He ﷺ said, "In paradise, there is a tent made from a single hollowed

106 Al-Zumar, 39:20.

107 Ustaz Zainul Abidin mentioned that this is how it is in A. Perhaps what was mentioned in Imām Aḥmad's *Musnad* is better: «فظننت أني أنا هو».

108 Jalāl al-Dīn al-Suyūṭī, *Al-Jāmi' al-ṣaghīr*, 5676; *Jam' al-Jawāmi'*, 14053/19. c.f. Al-Tirmidhi, #3688.

109 The hadith mentioned in al-Bukhārī and Muslim has the phrase «ستين» instead of «سبعين».

110 The word «للمؤمنين» is not included in the hadith.

pearl sixty *mīl*s wide.[111] There is a family [i.e. a wife] in each of the corners, for Muslims,[112] which cannot see the others [due to the distance], and a believer will visit [i.e. his families and enjoy] them."[113]

وَيَجِبُ الإِيْمَانُ بِالوِلْدَانِ، وَهُمْ فِي سِنِّ مَنْ هُوَ دُوْنَ البُلُوْغِ. وَالصَّحِيْحُ أَنَّهُمْ خُلِقُوْا فِي الجَنَّةِ لِخِدْمَةِ أَهْلِهَا مِنْ غَيْرِ وِلَادَةِ أَحَدٍ لَهُمْ، كَمَا خُلِقَتِ الحُوْرُ العِيْنُ كَذَلِكَ تَمَامًا لِنِظَامِهِمْ.

It is obligatory to believe in the youths. Their age [or at least their appearance] is of those who are adolescent. The sound opinion is that they were created in paradise to serve its inhabitants without anyone giving birth to them—just as the houris are created completely formed.

وَأَقَلُّ أَهْلِ الجَنَّةِ مَنْ يَخْدِمُهُ أَلْفُ غُلَامٍ، وَيُعْطَى فِي الجَنَّةِ قَدْرَ الدُّنْيَا عَشْرَ مَرَّاتٍ.

The least inhabitant of paradise is served by one thousand youths. In paradise, he is given the measure of this world tenfold.

---

111 One *mīl* equals 4,000 *dhirā'*, so 1.92 kilometres. So 60 *mīl*s equal 115.2 kilometres or 71.58 miles.

112 This clause ("for Muslims") is not part of the hadith,.

113 Al-Bukhārī, 4879; Muslim, 2838 #24; al-Tirmidhī, 2528; Jalāl al-Dīn al-Suyūṭī, *Al-Jāmi' al-ṣaghīr*, 7692; *Jam' al-Jawāmi'*, 17566/519. C.f. 'Abd al-Raḥmān al-Mubārakfūri, *Tuḥfat al-aḥwadhī* (Beirut: Dār al-Kutub al-'Ilmiyyah, 1353), #2528; al-Mullā 'Alī al-Qārī, *Mirqāt al-mafātīḥ sharḥ Moshkāt al-maṣābīḥ* (Lebanon: Dar al-Fikr, 2002/1422), #5616.

DESTINY AND DECREE [الإيمانُ بِالقَضاءِ وَالقَدرِ]

(١٥) وَوَاجِبٌ إِيْمَانُنَا بِالقَدَرِ * وَبِالقَضَا بِالنَّفْعِ وَبِالضَّرَرِ

(15) Our belief in destiny is obligatory * And in the decree, in benefit and in harm,

أَي: وَيَجِبُ عَلَى المُكَلَّفِ الإِيْمَانُ بِالقَضَاءِ وَالقَدَرِ.

Meaning: It is obligatory for the responsible person to believe in the decree [*al-qaḍā'*] and destiny [fate, foreordainment; *al-qadar*].[114]

فالقَدَرُ عِلمُهُ تَعَالَى أَزَلًا صِفَاتِ المَخْلُوْقَاتِ، فَكَانَ اللَّهُ تَعَالَى أَزَلًا يُحَدِّدُ كَلَّ مَخْلُوْقٍ بِحَدِّهِ الَّذِي يُوْجَدُ عَلَيْهِ حِيْنَ وُجُوْدِهِ مِنْ حُسْنٍ وَقُبْحٍ وَنَفْعٍ وَضُرٍّ.

Destiny is Allah's (Most High is He) eternal knowledge of the attributes of created beings. Allah, since eternity, determined what every entity will possess while it exists, including goodness, ugliness, benefit, and harm.[115]

والقَضَاءُ إِيْجَادُ اللَّهِ الأَشْيَاءَ مَعَ اتِّصَافِهَا بِالمَلَاحَةِ.

The decree is Allah bringing beings into existence with attributes of grace.[116]

---

114 *Jawharah*, 54; *Tuḥfah*, 354–56.
The definitions he gives here match what is given in *Jawharat al-tawḥīd* and follow the Māturīdī school. In some books, the author's definitions follow the Ash'arī school. For example, in *Qaṭar al-ghayth fī sharḥ Masā'il Abī Layth*, he defines *qaḍā'* as Allah's eternal will linked to things as they are, and *qadar* as Allah's bringing them into existence as they are in His knowledge.

115 *Jawharah*, 54; *Tuḥfah*, 357

116 *Jawharah*, 54; *Tuḥfah*, 357–58.

وَالإِيْمَـانُ بِهِمَا يَسْـتَدْعِي الرِّضَاءَ بِهِمَا، فَيَجِبُ الرِّضَـاءُ بِالقَضَاءِ وَالقَدَرِ بِـأَنْ لَا يَعْتَـرِضَ عَلَى اللَّهِ تَعَالَى فِي قَضَائِهِ وَقَدَرِهِ، وَيَعْتَقِدَ أَنَّ ذَلِكَ الأَمْرَ لِحِكْمَـةٍ وَإِنْ كُنَّـا لَا نَعْلَمُهَـا. وَهَـذَا قَدْ يُجَامِعُ عَدَمَ الرِّضَـاءِ بِالمَقْضِيِّ وَالمُقَدَّرِ بِأَنْ يَعْتَرِضَ عَلَى الكَافِرِ فِي اخْتِيَارِهِ الكُفْرَ وَاكْتِسَابِهِ لَهُ.

Believing in the two [i.e. decree and destiny] calls for being content with them both. Thus, it is obligatory to be content with the decree and destiny by not objecting to what Allah (Most High is He) has decreed and destined, and by believing that the matter is for a wise purpose even if we do not know [what] it [is]. This [contentment with the decree and destiny] could include a lack of contentment with the thing that has been decreed and fated in that one objects to a disbeliever for his choosing disbelief and acquiring it.[117]

وَرُوِيَ عَنْ عَلِيٍّ أَنَّهُ قَالَ: قَالَ رَسُوْلُ اللَّهِ ﷺ: «لَا يُؤْمِنُ عَبْدٌ حَتَّى يُؤْمِنَ بِأَرْبَعٍ: يَشْـهَدُ أَنْ لَا إِلَهَ إِلَّا اللَّهُ، وَأَنِّي رَسُـوْلُ اللَّهِ بَعَثَنِي بِالحَقِّ، وَيُؤْمِنُ بِالمَوْتِ، وَبِالبَعْثِ بَعْدَ المَوْتِ، وَيُؤْمِنُ بِالقَدَرِ خَيْرِهِ وَشَرِّهِ»، وَحُلْوِهِ وَمُرِّهِ.

It has been related that ʿAlī [﵁] said that the Messenger of Allah ﷺ said, "A servant does not believe until he believes in four: he testifies that there is no deity except Allah, and that I am the messenger of Allah and I was sent with the truth. And he believes in the resurrection after death. And he believes in destiny: good and evil,"[118] sweet and bitter.[119]

117 *Jawharah*, 54; *Tuḥfah*, 255.

118 Without the next two words: Al-Tirmidhī, 2145; al-Suyūṭī, *Al-Jāmiʿ al-ṣaghīr*, 13542; *Jamʿ al-jawāmiʿ*, 25794/1433. It is considered sound. cf Ibn Mājah, 81.

119 *Jawharah*, 54; *Tuḥfah*, 359.

SUPPLEMENTARY MATERIALS

[تَوابِعُ ثَلاثَةٌ لِلأَقسامِ المُتَقَدِّمَةِ]

هَـذَا مَـا يَتَعَلَّقُ بِالأَقْسَـامِ الثَّلَاثَةِ المُتَعَلِّقَةِ[120] بِمَسَـائِلِ هَذَا الفَنِّ. وَيَتْبَعُ ذَلِـكَ ثَلَاثَـةُ أَقْسَـامٍ أُخَرِ. الأَوَّلُ: مَـا يَجِبُ وُجُوْبَ اعْتِقَـادٍ. الثَّانِي: مَا يَجِبُ وُجُوْبَ مَعْرِفَةٍ. الثَّالِثُ: مَا يَجِبُ وُجُوْبَ عَمَلٍ.

This [i.e. what preceded] is what is related to the three sections connected to this art [i.e. matters related to the Divine and to the Prophets, and matters known through revelation].

Those [preceding matters] will be followed by three other sections:

a What is obligatory to be believed.
b What is obligatory to be known.
c What is obligatory to be performed.

وَقَدْ بَدَأْتُ بِالأَوَّلِ فَقُلْتُ:

I began with the first, and said:

120 Ustaz Zainul Abidin mentioned that A has «المتعلق», and perhaps what is mentioned here is better since it is an attribute of «الأقسام».

A. OBLIGATORY AS BELIEFS [قِسمُ ما يَجِبُ وُجوبَ اعتِقادٍ]

THE SERVANTS' ACTIONS [أَفْعالُ العِبادِ]

(١٦) ثُمَّ اعْتَقِدْ أَنَّ الخَلَائِقْ فِعْلَهَا * مَخْلُوقَةٌ لِلَّهِ لَا تَزِغْ لَهَا

(16) Then believe that created beings—their actions * Are created by Allah, so do not stray because of it

أي: يَجِبُ عَلَى المُكَلَّفِ اعْتِقَادُ أَنَّ اللَّهَ تَعَالَى خَلَقَ العِبَادَ وَأَعْمَالَهُمْ، وَأَنَّ كُلَّ مَا فِي الوُجُودِ مِمَّا سِوَى اللَّهِ تَعَالَى وَصِفَاتِهِ فَهُوَ فِعْلُ اللَّهِ وَخَلقِهِ، وَأَنَّ اللَّهَ مُنْفَرِدُ بِالتَّأْثِيرِ، وَأَنَّهُ لَا تَأْثِيرَ لِغَيرِ اللَّهِ فِي شَيْءٍ مَا، وَأَنَّ العَبْدَ لَيْسَ لَهُ فِي الفِعْلِ الاِخْتِيَارِيِّ إِلَّا مُجَرَّدُ الكَسْبِ -وَهُوَ مُقَارَنَةُ قُدْرَتِهِ لِلفِعْلِ-، وَبِسَبَبِهِ حَصَلَ التَّكْلِيْفُ.

It is obligatory for the responsible individual to believe that Allah (Most High is He) created [His] servants and their actions, and that everything existent other than Allah (Most High is He) and His attributes is an act of Allah and [it is] His creation.[121]

[It is obligatory to believe] that Allah alone has efficacy [i.e. the ability to produce an effect], and that nothing other than Allah has influence in anything.[122]

[It is obligatory to believe] that servants, when it comes to voluntary acts, have nothing except acquisition [*kasb*]. [Acquisition] is

121 *Jawharah*, 45; *Tuḥfah*, 290–93.
122 *Jawharah*, 45; *Tuḥfah*, 288.

one's capacity to act [*qudrah*] being concurrent with the act;[123] it [i.e. acquisition] is the reason for responsibility.[124]

وَيَجِبُ الِاعْتِقَادُ أَنَّ اللَّهَ تَعَالَى يَجُوزُ عَلَيْهِ خَلْقُ الخَيْرِ وَالشَّرِّ، وَأَنَّهُ لَا يَقَعُ فِي مُلْكِهِ إِلَّا مَا يُرِيْدُ، وَأَنَّه لَا يَجِبُ عَلَيْهِ لِعِبَادِهِ فِعْلُ الصَّلَاحِ وَالأَصْلَحِ.

It is obligatory to believe that it is possible for Allah (Most High is He) to create good and evil;[125] that nothing occurs in His kingdom except what He wills; and that it is not required for Him to do what is good and best for His slaves.[126]

قَوْلُهُ: «فَلَا تَزِغْ لَهَا»، أَي: لَا تَمِلْ عَنْ طَرِيْقِ أَهْلِ السُّنَّةِ لِهَذِهِ المَسْئَلَةِ.

His [the versifier's] saying, "do not stray because of it," means: "Do not stray from the path of Ahl al-Sunnah due to this issue."

وَقَدْ صَحَّ مَا قَالَ الأَشْعَرِيُّ وَسَائِرُ أَهْلِ السُّنَّةِ مِنْ أَنَّ لِلعَبْدِ مَشِيْئَةً تُسَمَّى كَسْبًا لَا تُؤْثِرُ إِلَّا بِمَشِيْئَةِ اللَّهِ تَعَالَى. وَانْتَفَى مَذْهَبُ القَدَرِيَّةِ الَّذِيْنَ يَقُوْلُوْنَ: «إِنَّا نَخْلُقُ أَفْعَالَنَا»، وَمَذْهَبُ الجَبَرِيَّةِ القَائِلِيْنَ: «لَا فِعْلَ لَنَا أَصْلًا».

What [Imām] al-Ash'arī and the rest of Ahl al-Sunnah have said (i.e. that the servant has a will—called "acquisition"—which[127] has no influence except through the will of Allah (Most High is He)) is sound.[128] The schools [*madhhabs*] of the Qadariyyah [free-willers] (who say that we create our own actions)[129] and the Jabariyyah

123 *Jawharah*, 48; *Tuḥfah*, 313.
124 *Jawharah*, 48; *Tuḥfah*, 317.
125 *Jawharah*, 45, 53; *Tuḥfah*, 293–53, 345.
126 *Jawharah*, 51–52; *Tuḥfah*, 333–44.
127 *Jawharah*, 48–50; *Tuḥfah*, 313–332.
128 *Jawharah*, 48; *Tuḥfah*, 318.
129 *Jawharah*, 48–49, 54; *Tuḥfah*, 319, 324, 355.

[predestinarians] (who say that we have no action at all) have been negated.[130]

وَمَثَّلَ المُلَّوِيُّ ذَلِكَ بِمَنْ يُرِيْدُ قَطْعَ بِطِّيْخَةٍ فَحَدَّدَ سِكِّيْنَةً وَهَيَّأَهَا وَأَوْجَدَ فِيْهَا أَسْبَابَ القَطْعِ وَأَزَالَ عَنْهَا مَوَانِعَهُ، ثُمَّ وَضَعَهَا عَلَى البِطِّيْخَةِ فَهِيَ لَا تَقْطَعُ دُوْنَ أَنْ يَتَحَامَلَ عَلَيْهَا التَّحَامُلَ المَعْرُوْفَ. وَلِذَلِكَ لَوْ وَضَعَ عَلَيْهَا مَا لَا يَصْلُحُ لِلقَطْعِ -كَحَطَبَةٍ مَثَلًا- لَمْ تَقْطَعْ وَلَوْ تَحَامَلَ، فَالعَبْدُ كَالسِّكِّيْنِ: خَلَقَهُ اللهُ تَعَالَى وَهَيَّأَهُ بِمَا أَعْطَاهُ مِنَ القُدْرَةِ لِلفِعْلِ.

Al-Mullawī likened this to someone who intends to cut a watermelon, so he sharpens a knife and prepares it, and he obtains the causes for the cutting and removes its obstructions. Next, he places the knife on the watermelon—but it will not cut without adequate pressure. This is why if something unfit for cutting (like wood, for example) is placed on it, it would not cut—not even if pressed. Thus, the servant is like the knife: Allah (Most High is He) created him and prepared him by giving him the [derived] power for the act.

فَمَنْ قَالَ: «أَنَا أَخْلُقُ فِعْلِي مُسْتَقِلًّا بِهِ» فَهُوَ كَمَنْ قَالَ: «السِّكِّيْنَ تَقْطَعُ بِمُجَرَّدِ وَضْعِهَا مِنْ غَيْرِ تَحَامُلٍ».

Whoever says that he creates his actions on his own is like the one who says that the knife will cut simply by being placed [i.e. upon the watermelon] without being pressed.

وَمَنْ قَالَ: «الفَاعِلُ هُوَ اللّٰهُ» مِنْ غَيْرِ نَظَرِ العَبْدِ أَصْلًا، كَمَنْ قَالَ: «هُوَ يَقْطَعُ البِطِّيْخَةَ بِتَحَامُلِ يَدِهِ أَوْ قَصْبَةٍ مَلْسَاءَ مِنْ غَيْرِ سِكِّيْنٍ».

Whoever says the actor is Allah (without considering the servant at all), is like someone who says that he cuts the watermelon by

130 *Jawharah*, 48; *Tuḥfah*, 317.

pressing his hand or a smooth reed without [involving] a knife.

وَالَّذِي يَقُوْلُ: «إِنَّهُ بَاشَرَ بِقُدْرَتِهِ المُهَيَّأَةِ لِفِعْلٍ يَخْلُقُهُ اللَّهُ تَعَالَى فِي ذَلِكَ الفِعْلِ» كَمَنْ قَالَ: «إِنَّ السِّكِّيْنَ قَطَعَتْ بِالتَّحَامُلِ عَلَيْهَا».

While the one who says that he exercised his capacity for an act that Allah (Most High is He) created in that act, is like someone who says that the knife cuts by being pressed upon.

بِهَذَا أَجْرَى عَلَيْهِ تَعَالَى عَادَتَهُ فِي النَّاسِ، لَوْ شَاءَ غَيْرَ ذَلِكَ فَعَلَ. وَهَذَا هُوَ الحَقُّ الَّذِي لَا شَكَّ فِيْهِ.

In this [way], Allah (Most High is He) imposes His norm upon people. If He so willed otherwise, He would do so. This is the truth of which there is no doubt.[131]

SEEING ALLAH, THE NIGHT JOURNEY, 'Ā'ISHAH'S INNOCENCE

[رُؤْيَةُ اللهِ تعالى - الإسراءُ والمِعراجُ - بَراءَةُ سَيِّدَتِنا عائِشَة]

(١٧) رُؤْيَةَ مَوْلَى ثُمَّ إِسْرَاءَ النَّبِي * بَرَاءَةً لِعَائِشَةْ مِنْ كَذِبِ

(17) Seeing our Lord during the Night Journey of our Prophet, * The innocence of 'Ā'ishah from lies

أَي: يَجِبُ اعْتِقَادُ أَنَّهُ تَعَالَى يُرَى بِالأَبْصَارِ فِي الآخِرَةِ لِلمُؤْمِنِيْنَ بِلَا تَكَيُّفٍ(132) لِلمَرْئِيِّ بِكَيْفِيَّةٍ مِنْ كَيْفِيَّاتِ الحَوَادِثِ مِنْ مُقَابَلَةٍ وَجِهَةٍ وَتَحَيُّزٍ وَغَيْرِ ذَلِكَ.

131 From "What [Imām] al-Ash'arī..." to here matches, almost verbatim, what is in al-Shirbīnī, *Al-Sirāj al-munīr*, 4:461–2.

132 A: «تكيّف»; TM: «كيف».

If is obligatory for us to believe that Allah (Most High is He) will be seen[133] via eyesight[134] in the afterlife, by believers, without being seen in a manner that created beings are seen (including facing, direction, occupying space, and other things).[135]

قَوْلُهُ: «رُؤْيَةَ» مَعْطُوفٌ عَلَى قَولِهِ: «أَنَّ الخَلَائِقَ».

Him [the versifier] saying "seeing" is grammatically connected (via a coordinating conjunction) to him saying "that created beings" [in the previous verse].

وَقَوْلُهُ: «ثَمَّ» اسْمُ إِشَارَةٍ لِلبَعِيْدِ، وَهُوَ الآخِرَةُ.

And "therein [*thamma*]" is a demonstrative pronoun for something distant, which [in this case] is the afterlife.

ويَجِبُ اعْتِقَادُ أَنَّهُ ﷺ أُسْرِيَ بِهِ لَيْلًا مِنْ مَكَّةَ إِلَى بَيْتِ المَقْدِسِ، وَأَنَّهُ عُرِجَ بِهِ مِنْهُ إِلَى السَّمَوَاتِ السَّبْعِ إِلَى سِدْرَةِ المُنْتَهَى إِلَى الكُرْسِيِّ إِلَى مُسْتَوًى سَمِعَ فِيْهِ صَرِيْفَ الأَقْلَامِ إِلَى العَرْشِ، وَأَنَّهُ كَلَّمَهُ رَبُّه فِي هَذِهِ اللَّيْلَةِ المُبَارَكَةِ وَرَأَى رَبَّهُ فِيْهَا بِعَيْنَي رَأْسِهِ رُؤْيَةً تَلِيْقُ بِهِ تَعَالَى.

It is obligatory to believe that he ﷺ journeyed at night from Mecca to Jerusalem, whence he ascended into the seven heavens to the lote tree at the most extreme limit [in the seventh heaven], [then] to the footstool, to a level where he could hear the scratching of the pens, and to the throne.[136]

[It is obligatory to believe] that he spoke to His Lord during this blessed night; and that he saw His Lord during it [this journey]

133 *Jawharah*, 55–56; *Tuḥfah*, 360–385.
134 *Jawharah*, 55; *Tuḥfah*, 364.
135 *Jawharah*, 55; *Tuḥfah*, 365.
136 *Jawharah*, 74; *Tuḥfah*, 482.

with the eyes in his head—seeing in a manner appropriate to Him (Most High is He).[137]

وَيَجِبُ اعْتِقَادُ بَرَاءَةِ أُمِّ الْمُؤْمِنِيْنَ عَائِشَةَ بِنْتِ أَبِي بَكْرٍ الصِّدِّيْقِ مِمَّا رَمَاهَا بِهِ الْمُنَافِقُوْنَ مِنْ أَشَدِّ الْكَذِبِ، وَالَّذِي خَاضَ فِيْهِ وَأَشَاعَهُ عَبْدُ اللّٰهِ بْنُ أُبَيٍّ بْنِ سَلُوْلَ رَأْسُ الْمُنَافِقِيْنَ، وَأُبَيٌّ اسْمُ أَبِيْهِ، وَسَلُوْلُ اسْمُ أُمِّهِ. وَقَدْ جَاءَ الْقُرْآنُ بِبَرَاءَتِهَا، فَمَنْ جَحَدَ بَرَاءَتَهَا أَوْ شَكَّ فِيْهَا كَفَرَ.

It is obligatory to believe that the Mother of the Believers 'Ā'ishah daughter of Abū Bakr al-Ṣiddīq [ﷺ] is innocent of the heinous slander the hypocrites spread about her.

The one who plunged into it and spread it is 'Abd Allah bin Ubayy bin Salūl, the leader of the hypocrites. ("Ubayy" being his father's name and "Salūl" being his mother's.)

The Quran declared her innocence.[138] Consequently, whoever denies her innocence or doubts it has disbelieved.[139]

وَحَاصِلُ قِصَّتِهَا أَنَّ النَّبِيَّ ﷺ كَانَ إِذَا أَرَادَ سَفَرًا أَقْرَعَ بَيْنَ نِسَائِهِ، فَلَمَّا أَرَادَ التَّوَجُّهَ لِغَزْوَةِ الْمُرَيْسِيْعِ أَقْرَعَ بَيْنَهُنَّ فَخَرَجَتِ الْقُرْعَةُ عَلَى عَائِشَةَ، فَتَوَجَّهَتْ مَعَهُ. فَفِي رُجُوْعِهِمْ مِنْهَا ضَاعَ عِقْدُهَا فَتَخَلَّفَتْ فِي طَلَبِهِ فَحُمِلَ هَوْدَجُهَا ظَنًّا أَنَّهَا فِيْهِ؛ لِأَنَّهَا كَانَتْ خَفِيْفَةً، وَسَارَ الْقَوْمُ. وَرَجَعَتْ إِلَيْهِمْ فَلَمْ تَجِدْهُمْ، فَمَكَثَتْ مَكَانَهَا فَأَخَذَهَا النَّوْمُ، فَمَرَّ بِهَا صَفْوَانُ

---

137 The Companions ﷺ disagreed whether the Prophet ﷺ saw Allah. 'Ā'ishah ﷺ denied it, while Ibn 'Abbās ﷺ affirmed it. The opinion presented in this text is preferred. One of the reasons for this preference is that when presented with otherwise equal evidence, the evidence that affirms has taken over the one that denies. *Jawharah*, 74; *Tuḥfah*, 482.

138 Al-Nūr, 24:11–20.

139 *Jawharah*, 74; *Tuḥfah*, 483–84.

بْـنُ المُعَطِّـلِ، وَكَانَ يَعْرِفُهَـا قَبْلَ آيَةِ الحِجَـابِ، وَكَانَ يَتَخَلَّفُ يَلْتَقِطُ مَا يَسْـقُطُ مِنَ المَتَاعِ. فَبَرَكَ نَاقَتَهُ وَوَلَّاهَا ظَهْرَهُ وَصَارَ يَسْـتَرْجِعُ جَهْرًا حَتَّى اسْـتَيْقَظَتْ، وَحَمَلَهَـا عَلَـى النَّاقَةِ وَلَمْ يَنْظُرْ إِلَيْهَا، وَقَادَ بِهَـا النَّاقَةَ مُوَلِّيَهَا ظَهْـرَهُ حَتَّـى أَدْرَكَ بِهَا النَّبِيَّ ﷺ. فَرَمَوْهَا بِهِ، وَفَشَـا ذَلِـكَ بَيْنَ المُنَافِقِيْنَ وَضُعَفَـاءِ المُسْـلِمِيْنَ، فَشَـقَّ ذَلِكَ عَلَى النَّبِيِّ ﷺ، فَأَنْـزَلَ اللَّهُ تَعَالَى فِي بَرَاءَتِهَا.

The gist of her story is that whenever the Prophet ﷺ intended to travel, he would draw lots between his wives [to determine who would accompany him]. Accordingly, when he intended to set out on the expedition to al-Muraysī'[140] [Banī Muṣṭalaq], he drew lots between them. 'Ā'ishah's lot was drawn, so she set out with him.

During the return, she misplaced her necklace and was delayed while looking for it. [While she had been looking,] they had placed her litter [*hawdaj*] [on her camel] thinking she was inside it since she was very light, and then set out. She returned to [the camp where she had left] them but did not find them. She stayed there and was overcome by sleep.

Ṣafwān bin al-Mu'aṭṭal passed by her. He knew her from before the verse of veiling.[141] He had been travelling behind the [returning] party in order to pick up whatever had dropped. He knelt his camel, turned his back to her, and began repeating, "Verily we belong to Allah, and verily unto Him we return [*innā li-Llāhi wa innā ilayhi rāji'ūn*]" aloud until she awoke. He loaded her on the camel without looking at her. He drove the camel with his back to her until bringing her to the Prophet ﷺ. They [the hypocrites] slandered her with it [adultery] and it [the slander] spread among the hypocrites

140 Al-Suyūṭī, *Al-Tawshīḥ sharḥ Al-Jāmi' al-ṣaḥīḥ* (Riyāḍ: Maktabat al-Rusdh, 1998/1419), 6:2568.

141 Al-Aḥzāb, 33:53.

and weak Muslims. This distressed the Prophet ﷺ and Allah (Most High is He) revealed her innocence.[142]

وَقَدْ كَانَتْ مِنْ أَفْضَلِ النِّسَاءِ. وَنَظَّمْتُ أَفْضَلِيَّةَ النِّسَاءِ أَخْذًا مِنْ قَوْلِ الشِّرْبِيْنِي، فَقُلْتُ:

She is among the best of women. [(May Allah be pleased with her and her father)]. I composed a verse concerning the best women, based on what al-Shirbīnī said.[143] I said:

فُضْلَى النِّسَاءِ مَرْيَمُ فَفَاطِمَةُ فَخَدِيْـ * ـجَةُ ثُمَّ عَائِشَةُ فَآسِيَّةُ فَاعْلَمَنَّ

The best of women are Maryam, then Fāṭimāh, then Khadī-
* -jah, next 'Ā'ishah, and then Āsiyah. So know this!

THE BEST OF CREATION IS OUR MASTER MUḤAMMAD ﷺ [أَفضَلُ خَلقِ اللهِ سَيِّدُنا مُحَمَّدٌ ﷺ]

(١٨) وَأَفْضَلُ الخَلْقِ مُحَمَّدٌ بِهِ * خَتْمُ رُسُلْ وَعَمَّ فِيْ بِعْثَتِهِ

(18) The best of creation is Muḥammad, through him * He sealed the messengers and universalised his sending

أَي: يَجِبُ اعْتِقَادُ أَنَّ سَيِّدَنَا مُحَمَّدًا ﷺ أَفْضَلُ المَخْلُوْقَاتِ جَمِيْعًا، وَيَلِيْهِ سَيِّدُنَا إِبْرَاهِيْمُ، ثُمَّ سَيِّدُنَا عِيْسَى، ثُمَّ سَيِّدُنَا نُوْحٌ -وَهَؤُلَاءِ أُوْلُوْ العَزْمِ-، ثُمَّ بَقِيَّةُ الرُّسُلُ. ثُمَّ الأَنْبِيَاءُ غَيْرُ الرُّسُلِ -وَهُمْ مُتَفَاضِلُوْنَ فِيْمَا بَيْنَهُمْ

142 From "The gist…": *Jawharah*, 74; *Tuḥfah*, 484.

143 Al-Shirbīnī, *Al-Sīrāj al-munīr*, 1:214, 3:260; *Mughnī al-muḥtāj* (Beirut: Dār al-Kutub al-'Ilmiyyah, 1994/1415), 4:202.

عِنْـدَ اللَّـهِ. ثُمَّ جِبْرِيْلُ، ثُمَّ مِيْكَائِيْلُ، ثُمَّ إِسْـرَافِيْلُ، ثُـمَّ عَزْرَائِيْلُ. ثُمَّ عَوَامُّ الْبَشَـرِ -وَهُـمْ أَوْلِيَاؤُهُـمْ كَأَبِي بَكْـرٍ وَعُمَرَ-، ثُمَّ عَـوَامُّ الْمَلَائِكَةِ -وَهُمْ غَيْرُ رُؤَسَـائِهِمْ الأَرْبَعَـةِ- وَهُمْ مُتَفَاضِلُوْنَ بَيْنَهُـم عِنْدَ اللَّهِ تَعَالَى وَذَلِكَ كَحَمَلَةِ الْعَرْشِ وَكَالْكَرُوْبِيِّيْنَ -وَهُمْ مَلَائِكَةٌ حَافُّوْنَ بِالْعَرْشِ طَائِفُوْنَ بِهِ.

It is obligatory to believe that our master Muḥammad ﷺ is the best of all creation.[144]

[Next are:]

- Our master Ibrāhīm
- Our master Mūsā
- Our master ʿĪsā
- Our master Nūḥ

These [five] are the ones of great determination and constancy [*ūlu l-ʿazm*].

[Next are:]

- The remaining messengers
- The prophets who were not messengers (having various degrees of superiority with Allah)

[They are followed by the four chief angels:]

- Jibrīl
- Mīkāʾīl
- Isrāfīl
- ʿAzrāʾīl

144 I have converted the paragraph into a bullet list.

[Then:]

- Common persons (with the best of them being Abū Bakr and then ʿUmar)
- Common angels (aside from their four leaders, with them having various degrees of superiority with Allah (Most High is He)); they include the bearers of the throne, and the *karūbiyyīn* who encircle and circumambulate the throne.[145]

يَجِبُ اعْتِقَـادُ أَنَّ نَبِيَّنَـا مُحَمَّـدًا ﷺ خَاتِمُ جَمِيْـعِ الأَنْبِيَاءِ، وَأَنَّـهُ لَا نَبِيَّ بَعْدَهُ.

It is obligatory to believe that our Prophet Muḥammad ﷺ is the seal of all of the Prophets, and that there is no prophet after him.[146]

وَيَجِبُ أَيْضًا اعْتِقَـادُ أَنَّ بِعْثَتَهُ عَامَّةٌ لِلإِنْسِ وَالجِنِّ عَلَى وَجْهِ التَّكْلِيْفِ، وَلِغَيْرِهِم عَلَى وَجْهِ التَّشْرِيْفِ،

It is also obligatory to believe that his being sent universally to humans and jinn is as a [deliverer of] religious duties,[147] and to all others as an honour [to them].[148]

وَأَنَّ شَرْعَهُ بَاقٍ إِلَى يَوْمِ القِيَامَةِ؛ لَا يَنْسَخُهُ شَرْعٌ آخَرُ لِعَدَمِ وُجُوْدِهِ بَعْدَهُ، وَأَنَّهُ وَقَعَ نَسْخُ بَعْضِ شَرْعِهِ بِبَعْضِهِ،

[It is obligatory to believe] that his legislation will remain [in effect] until Judgment Day without being abrogated by any other legislation since it [i.e. another legislation] does not exist after his [legislation].[149]

---

145 From the very beginning of the list: *Jawharah*, 67; *Tuḥfah*, 461. From the bearers of the throne: *Jawharah*, 78; *Tuḥfah*, 500.
146 *Jawharah*, 69; *Tuḥfah*, 467.
147 *Jawharah*, 69; *Tuḥfah*, 468.
148 *Jawharah*, 2; *Tuḥfah*, 26, 34.
149 *Jawharah*, 70; *Tuḥfah*, 70

[It is obligatory to believe] that parts of his legislation did abrogate other parts.[150]

وَأَنَّ مُعْجِزَاتَـهُ كَثِيْـرَةٌ كَرَدِّ عَيْنِ قَتَادَةَ حِيْنَ سَـالَتْ عَلَى وَجْهِهِ، وَشَـهَادَةِ الضَّبِّ بِنُبُوَّتِهِ، وَأَعْظَمُ المُعْجِزَاتِ القُرْآنُ العَظِيْمُ.

[It is obligatory to believe] that his miracles were numerous,[151] like returning Qatādah's eye when it protruded [from its socket] onto his face,[152] the spiny-tailed lizard [*ḍabb*] testifying to him being a prophet,[153] and—the greatest miracle of all—the Mighty Quran.[154]

150 *Jawharah*, 72; *Tuḥfah*, 475.
151 *Jawharah*, 73; *Tuḥfah*, 478.
152 c.f. Abū Bakr al-Bayhaqī, *Dalā'il al-nabuwwah* (Beirut: Dār al-Kutub al-'Ilmiyyah, 1405), 3:251.
153 c.f. ibid., 6:36.
154 These specific examples: *Jawharah*, 73; *Tuḥfah*, 480.

B. OBLIGATORY AS KNOWLEDGE [قِسمُ ما يَجِبُ وُجوبَ مَعرِفَةٍ]

ثُمَّ شَرَعَ النَّاظِمُ فِي القِسْمِ الثَّانِي مِنْ الأقسامِ التَّابِعَةِ، وَهُوَ وُجُوْبُ مَعْرِفَةٍ، أَي: إِقْرَارٍ وَانْقِيَادٍ، فَقَالَ:

The versifier then started the second supplement, which is what is obligatory as knowledge, i.e. to attest to and to comply to. He said:

THE TWENTY-FIVE PROPHETS ﷺ [مَعرِفَةُ الرُّسُلِ عليهم السلام]

(١٩) ثُمَّ اعْرِفِ الخَمْسَ وَعِشْرِيْنَ وَهُمْ * آدَمْ وَإِدْرِيْسُ وَنُوْحٌ هُوْدُ ثُمْ

(19) Then know the twenty-five [prophets] and they are * Ādam, Idrīs, and Nūḥ, Hūd, and then

(٢٠) صَالِحْ وَإِبْرَاهِيْمُ لُوْطٌ وَكَذَا * إِسْحَاقُ إِسْمَاعِيْلُ يَعْقُوْبُ احْتَذَى

(20) Ṣāliḥ, and Ibrāhīm, Lūṭ, and likewise * Isḥāq, Ismāʿīl, Yaʿqūb followed

(٢١) يُوْسُفْ وَأَيُّوْبُ شُعَيْبٌ مُوْسَى * هَارُوْنُ وَالْيَسَعْ وَذُو الكِفْلِ عَسَا

(21) Yūsuf, and Ayyūb, Shuʿayb, Mūsā * Hārūn, and al-Yasaʿ, and Dhu al-Kifl (who toughened)

(٢٢) دَاوُدُ نَجْلُهُ سُلَيْمَانُ اسْتَوَى * إِلْيَاسُ يُوْنُسُ زَكَرِيَّا يَحْيَى

(22) Dāwūd, his offspring Sulaymān was firm and steady * Ilyās, Yūnus, Zakariyyā, Yaḥyā

(٢٣) عِيْسَى مُحَمَّدٌ عَلَيْهِمُ السَّلَامْ * مِنَ الرَّحِيْمِ مَا بَقَى الأَيَّامْ[155]

(23) 'Īsā, Muḥammad upon whom be peace * From the Most Merciful so long as days remain

أَي: يَجِبُ مَعْرِفَةُ الخَمْسَةِ وَالعِشْرُوْنَ رَسُوْلًا[156] عَلَى التَّفْصِيْلِ؛ لِأَنَّهُمْ صَارُوْا مَعْلُوْمِيْنَ مِنَ الدِّيْنِ بِالضَّرُوْرَةِ.

It is obligatory to know the twenty-five messengers[157] specifically since they have become necessarily known as part of the religion.

وَيَكْفِي فِي الإِيْمَانِ بِكُلٍّ مِنْهُمْ أَنْ يَكُوْنَ بِحَيْثُ لَوْ سُئِلَ عَنْ رِسَالَتِهِ لَاعْتَرَفَ بِهَا، فَلَا يَجِبُ أَنْ يَسْرُدَهُمْ عَنْ حِفْظٍ.

What suffices for believing in each of them is that if one was asked about him being sent as a messenger, one would acknowledge it. It is not obligatory that one can list them from memory.

وَمَنْ أَنْكَرَ وَاحِدًا مِنْهُمْ بَعْدَ أَنْ عَلِمَهُ كَفَرَ، بِخِلَافِ مَا لَوْ سُئِلَ عَنْهُ ابْتِدَاءً فَقَالَ: «لَا أَعْرِفُهُ»، فَلَا يَكْفُرُ.

Anyone who denies one of them, after learning of him [being a prophet], has disbelieved. This is in contrast to if he had been asked about him initially [i.e. prior to being informed] and said, "I do not know him," for in that case he would not have disbelieved.[158]

---

155 This is as it is in A and R have. Ustaz Zainul Abidin suggests «مِنَ الرَّحِيْمِ مَا بَقِيْ مِنَ الأَيَّامْ», though «مِنَ الرَّحِيْمِ مَا تَبَقَّى الأَيَّامْ» is also better.

156 Ustaz Zainul Abidin mentioned that A has «رسلًا», and perhaps what is mentioned here is better.

157 In this section, the author lists all of the prophets we are required to know and not just those sent with revealed legislation. And Allah knows best.

158 *Jawharah*, 18; *Tuḥfah*, 115.

[They are:]

أَوَّلُهُمْ آدَمُ أَبُ الْبَشَرِ صَفِيُّ اللّٰهِ وَكَانَ رَسُوْلًا إِلَى أَوْلَادِهِ.

1 Ādām. The father of humanity, friend of Allah. He was sent as a messenger to his children.

وَثَانِيهُم إِدْرِيْسُ بْنُ شِيْثِ بْنِ آدَمَ، وَاسْمُهُ أَخْنُوْخُ، وَهُوَ أَوَّلُ نَبِيٍّ بُعِثَ مِنْ بَنِي آدَمَ عَلَيْهِ السَّلَامُ.

2 Idrīs son of Shīth son of Ādām. His name is Akhnūkh. He is the first prophet sent from amongst the children of Ādām ﷺ.

وَثَالِثُهُمْ نُوحٌ الَّذِي نَجَّاهُ اللّٰهُ مِنَ الغَرَقِ فِي السَّفِيْنَةِ، وَاسْمُهُ شَاكِرٌ. وَكَانَ أَوَّلُ مَنْ أُمِرَ بِنَسْخِ الأَحْكَامِ وَأُمِرَ بِالشَّرَائِعِ، وَكَانَ قَبْلَهُ نِكَاحُ الأُخْتِ مُبَاحًا وَحُرِّمَ ذَلِكَ عَلَى عَهْدِهِ.

3 Nūḥ. Whom Allah saved from the flood using an ark. His name is Shākir. He was the first [prophet] sent to abrogate rulings and to command [following revealed] legislations. Before him, marrying one's sister was permissible; during his time, it was declared unlawful.

وَرَابِعُهُمْ هُوْدٌ الَّذِي نَجَّاهُ اللّٰهُ مِنَ الرِّيحِ الَّتِي أَهْلَكَتْ الكَافِرِيْنَ، قَوْمِ عَادٍ اسْمُ مُلْكِهِمْ. عَذَّبَهُمْ بِهَا سَبْعَ لَيَالٍ وَثَمَانِيَةَ أَيَّامٍ، تَدْخُلُ فِي مَنَاخِرِهِمْ وَتَخْرُجُ مِنْ أَدْبَارِهِمْ، وَتَرْفَعُهُمْ وَتَضْرِبُهُمْ عَلَى الأَرْضِ عَلَى وُجُوْهِهِمْ حَتَّى صَارُوْا كَأُصُوْلِ نَخْلٍ خَاوِيَةٍ.

4 Hūd. Allah saved him from the flood winds that destroyed the disbelievers of the people of 'Ād (the name of their kingdom). For seven nights and eight days He punished them with the wind: it

would enter their nostrils and exit their rears; it would lift them up and smash their faces into the ground until they became like the hollow trunks of palm trees.

وَخَامِسُهُمْ صَالِحٌ الَّذِي نَجَّاهُ اللَّهُ تَعَالَى مِنَ الصَّيْحَةِ الَّتِي أَهْلَكَتْ الكَافِرِيْنَ، وَهُوَ قَوْمُ ثَمُوْدَ، وَهُوَ اسْمُ بِئْرٍ بِأَرْضِ الحِجْرِ. صَاحَ جِبْرِيْلُ بِهِمْ صَيْحَةً وَاحِدَةً فَهَلَكُوْا جَمِيْعًا أَوْ أَتَتْهُمْ صَيْحَةٌ مِنَ السَّمَاءِ فَتَقَطَّعَتْ قُلُوْبُهُمْ فِي صُدُوْرِهِم فَمَاتُوْا جَمِيْعًا.

5 Ṣāliḥ. Allah (Most High is He) saved him from the awful shriek that destroyed the disbelieving people of Thamūd (which is the name of a well in the land of Ḥijr). [Either] Jibrīl called out a single shriek and destroyed them in their entirety; or a single shriek came from the heavens and cut their hearts from their chests causing them all to die.

وَسَادِسُهُمْ إِبْرَاهِيْمُ الَّذِي نَجَّاهُ اللَّهُ تَعَالَى مِنْ نَارِ نُمْرُوْذَ(159).

6 Ibrāhim. Allah saved him from the fire of Numrūd.

وَسَابِعُهُمْ لُوْطُ بْنُ هَارَانَ أَخِي إِبْرَاهِيْمَ -وَقِيْلَ: إِنَّ لُوْطًا ابْنُ عَمِّ إِبْرَاهِيْمَ- الَّذِي نَجَّاهُ اللَّهُ تَعَالَى مِنَ العَذَابِ الَّذِي أَهْلَكَ الكَافِرِيْنَ، رُوِيَ أَنَّ جِبْرِيْلَ أَدْخَلَ جَنَاحَهُ تَحْتَ قُرَى قَوْمِ لُوْطٍ. وَكَانَتْ خَمْسَ مَدَائِنَ، وَفِيْهَا أَرْبَعمِائَةِ أَلْفٍ. فَرَفَعَ المَدَائِنَ كُلَّهَا حَتَّى سَمِعَ أَهْلُ السَّمَاءِ صِيَاحَ الدِّيْكَةِ وَنَهِيْقَ الحَمِيْرِ وَنُبَاحَ الكِلَابِ، لَمْ يُكْفَأْ لَهُمْ إِنَاءٌ وَلَمْ يَنْتَبِهْ نَائِمٌ، ثُمَّ اسْقَطَهَا مَقْلُوْبَةً إِلَى الأَرْضِ، ثُمَّ أَمْطَرَ اللَّهُ عَلَيْهَا حِجَارَةً مِنْ طِيْنٍ طُبِخَ بِالنَّارِ.

159 Ustaz Zainul Abidin mentioned that A has «نمروذ», and perhaps what is mentioned here is better.

7 Lūṭ son of Hārān the brother of Ibrāhīm. (Another opinion is that Lūṭ is the son of the paternal uncle of Ibrāhīm). Allah (Most High is He) saved him from the torture that destroyed the disbelievers. It was narrated that Jibrīl inserted his wing below the villages of the people of Lūṭ (which were five cities containing four-hundred thousand [people]), and lifted the towns completely until the people of the heavens heard the roosters crowing, donkeys braying, and dogs barking; [he did this gently,] without containers overturning or waking those asleep. They were then dropped upside down to the ground, after which Allah rained stones of fire-baked clay upon them.

وَثَامِنُهُمْ إِسْحَاقُ بْنُ إِبْرَاهِيْمَ مِنْ سَارَةَ أُخْتِ لُوْطٍ.

8 Isḥāq son of Ibrāhīm (and Sārah the sister of Lūṭ).

وَتَاسِعُهُمْ إِسْمَاعِيْلُ بْنُ إِبْرَاهِيْمَ مِنْ هَاجَرَ.

9 Ismā'īl son of Ibrāhīm (and Hājar).

وَعَاشِرُهُمْ يَعْقُوْبُ بْنُ إِسْحَقَ، وَسُمِّيَ يَعْقُوْبُ بِـ«إِسْرَائِيْلَ» أَيْضًا، وَسُمِّيَ بِذَلِكَ لِأَنَّهُ وَالعِيْصَ كَانَا تَوْأَمَيْنِ؛ فَتَقَدَّمَ عِيْصُ فِي الخُرُوْجِ مِنْ بَطْنِ أُمِّهِ وَخَرَجَ يَعْقُوْبُ عَقِبَهُ.

10 Ya'qūb son of Isḥāq. Ya'qūb is also named "Isrā'īl" because he and al-'Īṣ were twins; 'Īṣ was born first, and Ya'qūb followed him immediately after.

وَقَوْلُهُ: «احْتَذَى»، أَي: اقْتَدَى يَعْقُوْبُ مَنْ تَقَدَّمَ عَلَيْهِ فِي الذِّكْرِ، وَاقْتَدَى بِالعِيْصِ؛ كَمَا رُوِيَ أَنَّ العِيْصَ قَالَ: «أَنَا أَخْرَجُ مِنْ بَطْنِ أُمِّي أَوَّلًا»، قَالَ يَعْقُوْبُ: «أَنَا أَخْرُجُ أَوَّلًا»، فَقَالَ العِيْصُ: «إِنْ كُنْتَ تَخْرُجُ

أَوَّلًا أَنَا أَشُــقُّ بَطْنَ أُمِّي»، فَقَالَ يَعْقُوبُ: «إِذًا أُخْرُجْ أَنْتَ وَأَنَا عَقِبُكَ»، وَأُمُّهُمَا تَسْمَعُ كَلَامَهُمَا. وَلِأَجْلِ ذَلِكَ سُمِّيَ أَوَّلُ الخَارِجِ بِـ«عِيْصٍ».

Him [the versifier] saying "followed [*iḥtadhā*]," i.e. Yaʿqūb came after the ones mentioned before him and followed al-ʿĪṣ, just as it was related that al-ʿĪṣ said, "I will exit from my mother's womb first." Yaʿqūb said, "In that case, I will exit first." So al-ʿĪṣ said, "If you exit first, I will split my mother's womb." Yaʿqūb then said, "In that case, exit first and I will be right behind you." Their mother heard their conversation, and because of that the first to exit was named "ʿĪṣ."[160]

وَحَادِيَ عَشَرِهِمْ يُوْسُفُ بْنُ يَعْقُوْبَ.

11 Yūsuf son of Yaʿqūb.

وَثَانِيَ عَشَرِهِمْ أَيُّوْبُ بْنُ آمُوْصَ.

12 Ayyūb son of Āmūṣ.

وَثَالِثَ عَشَرِهِمْ شُعَيْبُ بْنُ نُوَيْبَ الَّذِي نَجَّاهُ اللَّهُ مِنَ الصَّيْحَةِ الَّتِي أَهْلَكَتْ الكَافِرِيْنَ مِنْ أَهْلِ مَدْيَنَ. صَاحَ جِبْرِيْلُ بِهِمْ صَيْحَةً خَرَّجَتْ أَرْوَاحَهُمْ وَمَاتُوْا جَمِيْعًا، وَقِيْلَ: أَتَتْهُمْ صَيْحَةٌ مِنَ السَّمَاءِ. قَالَ ابْنُ عَبَّاسٍ: «لَمْ يُعَذِّبِ اللَّهُ تَعَالَى أُمَّتَيْنِ بِعَذَابٍ إِلَّا قَوْمَ شُعَيْبٍ وَقَوْمَ صَالِحٍ؛ فَأَمَّا قَوْمُ صَالِحٍ فَأَخَذَتْهُمُ الصَّيْحَةُ مِنْ تَحْتِهِم، وَأَمَّا قَوْمُ شُعَيْبٍ فَأَخَذَتْهُمُ الصَّيْحَةُ مِنْ فَوْقِهِمْ.

160 The name "Yaʿqūb" is derived from *ʿaqb* which means to come after. Opinions regarding "ʿĪṣ" include that it is derived from *ʿṣā* which means to oppose, resist, disobey; that "ʿIṣ" is from *ʿisā,* meaning hairy or rough; or that it is a foreign word meaning redness.

13 Shu'ayb son of Nuwayb. Allah saved him from the shrieking that destroyed the people of Madyan. Jibrīl called out a single shriek that removed their souls [from their bodies] and they all died. Another opinion is that a shriek came down from the sky. Ibn 'Abbās said, "Allah (Most High is He) did not punish two nations with a single punishment except for the people of Shu'ayb and the people of Ṣāliḥ."[161]

The shriek took the people of Ṣāliḥ from below and the people of Shu'ayb from above.

وَرَابِعَ عَشَرِهِمْ مُوْسَى بْنُ عِمْرَانَ.

14 Mūsā son of 'Imrān.

وَخَامِسَ عَشَرِهِمْ هَارُوْنُ أَخُوْ مُوْسَى أَكْبَرُ عَنْهُ سَنَةً(162).

15 Hārūn. Brother of Mūsā and older by one year.

وَسَادِسَ عَشَرِهِمْ اليَسَعُ، وَهُوَ أُخْطُوْبُ(163) بْنُ العَجُوْزِ، وَكَانَ اليَسَعُ تِلْمِيْذَ إِلْيَاسَ وَخَلِيْفَةً مِنْ بَعْدِهِ.

16 Al-Yasa'. He is Ukhṭūb, the son of the elder. Al-Yasa' was the student of Ilyās and his successor.

وَسَابِعَ عَشَرِهِمْ ذُوْ الكِفْلِ. قَالَ عَطَاءٌ: «سُمِّيَ بِذَلِكَ لِأَنَّ نَبِيًّا مِنْ أَنْبِيَاءِ بَنِي إِسْرَائِيْلَ أَوْحَى اللَّهُ تَعَالَى إِلَيْهِ: ‹أَنِّي أُرِيْدُ أَنْ أَقْبِضَ رُوْحَكَ، فَاعْرِضْ مُلْكَكَ عَلَى بَنِي إِسْرَائِيْلَ؛ فَمَنْ تَكَفَّلَ لَكَ أَنْ يُصَلِّيَ بِاللَّيْلِ وَلَا يَفْتُرُ، وَيَصُوْمَ بِالنَّهَارِ وَلَا يُفْطِرُ، وَيَقْضِيَ بَيْنَ النَّاسِ وَلَا يَغْضَبُ، فَادْفَعْ مُلْكَكَ

161 Al-Shirbīnī, *Al-Sirāj al-munīr*, 2:77.

162 This is as it is in the various printed editions. Perhaps «منه بسنة» is better.

163 Ustaz Zainul Abidin mentioned this is how it is in A. Perhaps «هو ابن أخطوب»—with «ابن» before «أخطوب»—is better.

إِلَيْهِ). فَفَعَلَ ذَلِكَ،فَقَالَ شَابٌّ: (أَنَا أَتَكَفَّلُ لَكَ بِهَذَا). فَتَكَفَّلَ وَوَفَّى بِهِ، فَشَكَرَ اللَّهَ لَهُ وَنَبَّأَهُ فَسُمِّيَ ذَا الكِفْلِ». قِيْلَ: إِنَّ الَّذِي اسْتَخْلَفَهُ هُوَ الْيَسَعُ.

17 Dhu al-Kifl. 'Aṭā' said he was named that because Allah (Most High is He) revealed to one of the prophets of Banī Isrā'īl: "I want to take your soul, so offer your kingdom to Banī Isrā'īl. Whoever pledges to you that he will take responsibility to pray at night without ceasing, fast all day without breaking, judge cases between people and not get angry, then give your kingdom to him." He did this, and a young man said, "I pledge to you to take responsibility for this." He [the young man] pledged to take the responsibility and fulfilled it, so Allah thanked him for it and He elevated him, and named him "Dha al-Kifl (he who pledged to bear responsibilities)." Another opinion is that al-Yasa' was the one who appointed him as successor.

قَوْلُهُ: «عَسَا»، أَي: اشْتَدَّ ذُوْ الكِفْلِ لِمَا قِيْلَ إِنَّهُ رَجُلٌ كَفَلَ أَنْ يُصَلِّيَ كُلَّ لَيْلَةٍ مِائَةَ رَكْعَةٍ إِلَى أَنْ يَقبِضَهُ اللَّهُ تَعَالَى، فَوَفَّى بِهِ.

Him [the versifier] saying, "who toughened [*'asā*]," i.e. Dhu al-Kifl became tough because of what was said concerning him being a man who pledged that he would pray one-hundred prayer-cycles every night until Allah (Most High is He) took him, and he fulfilled it.

وَثَامِنَ عَشَرِهِمْ دَاوُدُ بْنُ إِيْشَا.

18 Dāwūd son of Īshā.

تَاسِعَ عَشَرِهِمْ سُلَيْمَانُ؛ وَهُوَ ابْنُ دَاوُدَ. وَهُمَا الَّذَانِ بَنَيَا بَيْتَ المَقْدِسِ بِأَمْرِ اللَّهِ تَعَالَى؛ دَاوُدَ بِخَطِّهِ وَتَأْسِيْسِهِ، وَسُلَيْمَانَ بِإِكْمَالِهِ وَتَشْيِيْدِهِ.

19 Sulaymān son of Dāwūd. The two of them built Jerusalem following Allah's command to Dāwūd to design and to begin its construction, and to Sulaymān to complete and plaster it.

وَقَوْلُـهُ: «اسْـتَوَى»، أَي: عَدَلَ سُـلَيْمَانُ فِي الحُكْـمِ وَقَهَرَ عَلَى المُلْكِ، وَكَانَ سُلَيْمَانُ مِمَّنْ آتَاهُ اللَّهُ المُلْكَ وَالنُّبُوَّةَ كَأَبِيْهِ.

Him [the versifier] saying, "firm and steady [*istawā*]," i.e. Sulaymān was just in ruling and he prevailed as a sovereign.

Sulaymān was among those who Allah gave both sovereignty and prophethood—just like his father.

وعِشْرُوْهُمْ[164] إِلْيَاسُ بْنُ يَاسِيْنَ مِنْ سِبْطِ يُوْشَعَ بْنِ نُوْنٍ، بَعَثَهُ اللَّهُ تَعَالَى إِلَى أَهْلِ بَعَلْبَكَ.

20 Ilyās son of Yāsīn. He was a grandchild of Yūshaʿ son of Nūn. Allah (Most High is He) sent him to the people of Baʿalbak.

وَالحَادِي وَالعِشْـرُوْنَ يُوْنُسُ بْنُ مَتَّى، بَعَثَهُ اللَّهُ تَعَالَى إِلَى أَهْلِ نِيْنَوَى مِنْ قُرَى المَوْصِلِ.

21 Yūnus son of Mattā. Allah (Most High is He) sent him to the people of Nīnawā, a village in Mawṣil.

وَالثَّانِي وَالعِشْرُوْنَ زَكَرِيَّا بْنُ أَدْنَ.

22 Zakariyyā son of Adn.

وَالثَّالِثُ وَالعِشْرُوْنَ يَحْيَى بْنُ زَكَرِيَّا.

23 Yaḥyā son of Zakariyyā.

164 This is how all editions have it.

وَالرَّابِعُ وَالعِشْرُوْنَ عِيْسَى ابْنُ(165) مَرْيَمَ بِنْتِ عِمْرَانَ.

24 'Īsā son of Maryam daughter of 'Imrān.

وَالخَامِسُ وَالعِشْرُوْنَ سَيِّدُنَا مُحَمَّدٌ خَاتَمُ الأَنْبِيَاءِ وَالمُرسَلِيْنَ صَلَّى اللَّهُ عَلَيْهِ وَسَلَّمَ عليهِمْ أَجْمَعِيْنَ.

25 Our master Muḥammad, the seal of the prophets and messengers (may Allah bless him and may peace be upon them all).

قَوْلُهُ: «مَا بَقِيَ الأَيَّامُ»، أَيِ: الأَوْقَاتُ.

Him [the versifier] saying, "so long as days remain [*mā baqiya l-ayyām*]," i.e. time.

THE ANGELS [مَعرِفَةُ المَلائِكَةِ رِضوانُ اللهِ عَلَيهِم]

(٢٤) ثُمَّ اعْرِفِ العَشَرَةَ بِالتَّحْقِيْقِ * جِبْرِيْلُ مِيْكَائِلُ قَاسِمْ رِزْقِ

(24) Then know the ten [angels] in detail * Jībrīl, Mīkā'īl the divider of sustenance,

(٢٥) فِي اللَّوْحِ إِسْرَافِيْلُ عَزْرَائِيْلُ * رِضْوَانُ مَالِكٌ رَقِيْبُ الكَامِلُ

(25) In the Tablet, Isrāfīl, 'Azrā'īl, * Riḍwān, Mālik, Raqīb the complete

165 A: «بن». Perhaps «ابن» would be better since the next person named is not the biological father of the previous. (And Allah knows best.)

(٢٦) عَتِيْدُ مُنْكَرٌ وَنَكِيْرٌ قَبْلَهُمَا * رُوْمَانُ نَاكُوْرٌ فَقِيْلَ مَعْهُمَا

(26) 'Atīd, Munkar, and Nakīr before them both * Rūmān, Nākūr, and it's said [he's] with them both

أَيْ: يَجِبُ مَعْرِفَةُ العَشَرَةِ مِنَ المَلَائِكَةِ تَفْصِيْلًا، وَهُمْ:

It is obligatory to know ten angels specifically.[166] They are:[167]

جِبْرِيْلُ: مُوَكَّلٌ بِالوَحْيِ.

1   Jibrīl. The one entrusted with revelation.

وَمِيْكَائِيْلُ: مُوَكَّلٌ بِكَيْلِ الأَمْطَارِ وَالبِحَارِ وَالأَنْهَارِ وَالأَرْزَاقِ، وَتَصْوِيْرِ الأَجِنَّةِ وَالأَرْحَامِ.

2   Mikā'īl. The one entrusted with measuring out rains, oceans, rivers, sustenance, and forming foetuses and wombs.[168]

وَإِسْرَافِيْلُ: مُوَكَّلٌ بِاللَّوْحِ المَحْفُوْظِ، وَالنَفْخِ فِي الصُّوْرِ لِلإِمَاتَةِ ثُمَّ لِلإِحْيَاءِ.

3   Isrāfil. The one entrusted with the protected tablet, and blowing in the trumpet which causes death and the resurrection.

وَعَزْرَائِيْلُ: مُوَكَّلٌ بِقَبْضِ الأَرْوَاحِ لِجَمِيْعِ المَخْلُوْقَاتِ وَلَوْ بَعُوْضَةً.

4   'Azrā'īl. The one entrusted with grasping every creature's soul (even a mosquito's).[169]

---

166   *Jawharah*, 18; *Tuḥfah*, 115.
167   Translator added numbers and formatted them as an enumerated list.
168   Translated as it is in the book.
169   *Jawharah*, 88; *Tuḥfah*, 570.

وَرِضْوَانُ: خَازِنُ الجَنَّةِ.

5 Riḍwān. The guardian of Paradise.

وَمَالِكٌ: خَازِنُ النَّارِ.

6 Mālik. The guardian of hellfire.

وَرَقِيبٌ وَعَتِيدٌ: وَهُمَا يَكْتُبَانِ عَمَلَ المُكَلَّفِ مِنْ الثَّقَلَيْنِ. فَرَقِيبٌ عَنْ يَمِيْنِ المُكَلَّفِ يَكْتُبُ الحَسَنَاتِ عَقِبَ فِعْلِهِ فَوْرًا، وَهُوَ أَمِيْرٌ أَوْ أَمِيْنٌ عَلَى مَنْ فِي اليَسَارِ. وَعَتِيدٌ عَنْ شِمَالِهِ يَكْتُبُ السَّيِّئَاتِ. فَإِنْ عَمِلَ العَبْدُ سَيِّئَةً قَالَ لِلأَمِيْنِ: «أَكْتُبُ؟»، فَيَقُوْلُ: «دَعْهُ سَبْعَ سَاعَاتٍ، لَعَلَّهُ يَتُوْبُ». فَإِذَا لَمْ يَتُبْ قَالَ: «نَعَمْ، أُكْتُبْ. أَرَاحَنَا اللهُ مِنْهُ»، وَهُوَ دُعَاءٌ عَلَيْهِ بِالمَوْتِ.

7–8 Raqīb and ʿAtīd. The recorders of acts for [legally] responsible humans and jinn.

Raqīb is on the individual's right and records good deeds immediately upon their performance. He is the leader or secretary of the one to the left.

ʿAtīd is to his left and records bad deeds. If the servant does a bad act, he says to the secretary, "Do I record it?," and he [Raqīb] replies, "Leave him for seven hours; perhaps he will repent." If he does not repent, he [Raqīb] replies, "Affirmative. Write it. May Allah relieve us of him!," which is a supplication for his death.[170]

وَقَالَ ابْنُ جُرَيْجٍ: «هُمَا مَلَكَانِ أَحَدُهُمَا عَنْ يَمِيْنِ بَنِي آدَمَ وَالآخَرُ عَنْ يَسَارِهِ، فَالَّذِي عَنْ يَمِيْنِهِ يَكْتُبُ بِغَيْرِ شَهَادَةِ صَاحِبِهِ، وَالَّذِي عَنْ يَسَارِهِ لَا يَكْتُبُ إِلَّا بِشَهَادَةِ صَاحِبِهِ».

170 For the two angels: *Jawharah*, 85; *Tuḥfah*, 549–50.

Ibn Jurayj said, "They are two angels, one on the right of the Children of Ādam and the other on his left. The one on his right records without his companion witnessing it. The one on the left does not record except with his companion witnessing."

فَيُكَفَّرُ مُنْكِرُ وَاحِدٍ مِنْ هَؤُلَاءِ.

Someone who rejects one of those [aforementioned eight angels] is judged a disbeliever.

وَأَمَّا نَكِيرٌ وَمُنْكَرٌ فَلَا يُكَفَّرُ مُنْكِرُهُمَا لِأَنَّهُ اخْتُلِفَ فِي أَصْلِ السُّؤَالِ. كَذَا قَالَ شَيْخُنَا يُوسُفُ فِي «فَتْحِ القَادِرِ المُرِيْدِ». وَهُمَا يَسْأَلَانِ المَيِّتَ المُكَلَّفَ مِنَ الثَّقَلَيْنِ عَنْ التَّوْحِيْدِ وَالدِّيْنِ. وَهُمَا لِلْمُؤْمِنِ الطَّائِعِ وَغَيْرِهِ. قِيْلَ: وَمَعَهُمَا مَلَكٌ آخَرُ يُقَالُ لَهُ «نَاكُوْرٌ»، وَقِيْلَ: يَجِيْءُ قَبْلَهُمَا رُوْمَانُ.

9–10 As for Nakīr and Munkar: Someone who rejects them is not judged a disbeliever since there is disagreement concerning the very same questioning.[171] (This is what our shaykh Yūsuf said in *Fatḥ al-qādir al-murīd.*)[172]

These two [Nakīr and Munkar] ask responsible individuals (humans and jinn) who have died about monotheism and religion. They [ask] obedient believers and others. Another opinion is that there is another angel with them who is said to be Nākūr. And another opinion is that Rūmān comes before them.

وَيَكُوْنُ السُّؤَالُ بَعْدَ تَمَامِ الدَّفْنِ وَعِنْدَ انْصِرَافِ النَّاسِ.

---

171 *Jawharah*, 18, 96; *Tuḥfah*, 115, 609.

172 Shaykh Yūsuf is Yūsuf al-Sanbalawaynī al-Sharqāwī (d1285AH). Our author repeats the same statement in several of his other works, with this attribution. Shaykh Ibrāhīm al-Bājūrī mentions it in *Jawharat al-tawḥīd*, minus the attribution (*Jawharah*, 18; *Tuḥfah*, 115). See Abū Ḥasan al-Ash'arī, *Maqālāt al-islāmiyyīn* (n.p.: Al-Maktabah al-'Aṣriyyah, 1426/2005), 2:354 #214.

The questioning takes place after burial has completed and people have left.[173]

وَمَـنْ عَدَا هَـؤُلَاءِ مِنَ المَلَائِكَةِ تَجِبُ مَعْرِفَتُهُمْ إِجْمَالًا بِأَنْ يَعْتَقِدَ أَنَّ لِلَّهِ مَلَائِكَـةً لَا يَعْلَـمُ عَدَدَهُـمْ إِلَّا هُـوَ، وَكَمَا قَالَ تَعَالَى: ﴿وَمَـا يَعْلَمُ جُنُودَ رَبِّكَ إِلَّا هُوَ﴾.

As for other angels: It is obligatory to know about them overall in that one believes that Allah has angels whose number is known only to Him, just as He Most High has said, "And none knows the soldiers of your Lord except Him."[174]

THE SCRIPTURES [مَعرِفَةُ الكُتُبِ وَالصُّحُفِ]

(٢٧) وَاعْرِفْ صُحُفْ مُوْسَى وَإِبْرَهِيْمْ(175) كَذَا * تَـوْرَاةٌ إِنْجِيْلٌ زَبُـوْرٌ فَاحْتَذَى

(27) Know the scriptures of Mūsā, and Ibrāhīm likewise, * Torah, Gospels, Psalms, following

(٢٨) قُـرْآنٌ ثُـمَّ غَـيْرُهَـا بِالجُمْلَةِ * وَاعْرِفْ لِأَنْسَابِ النَّبِيْ وَصُوْرَةِ

(28) Quran, then others in general * And know the lineage of the Prophet and appearance

أَي: يَجِبُ مَعْرِفَةُ صُحُفِ سَيِّدِنَا إِبْرَاهِيْمَ وَسَيِّدِنَا مُوْسَى، قَالَ اللَّهُ تَعَالَى: ﴿إِنَّ هَذَا لَفِي الصُّحُفِ الْأُوْلَى * صُحُفِ إِبْرَاهِيْمَ وَمُوْسَى﴾، أَي: أَنَّ مَعْنَى هَذَا الكَلَامِ فِي صُحُفِ إِبْرَاهِيْمَ وَمُوْسَى.

173 *Jawharah*, 96; *Tuḥfah*, 607.

174 Al-Muddaththir, 74:31.

175 This is as all editions have it, though «أَبْرَهَمْ» would be better for the metre.

It is obligatory to know of the scriptures of our master Ibrāhīm and our master Mūsā. Allah (Most High is He) says, "Indeed, this is in the former scriptures; the scriptures of Ibrāhīm and Mūsā,"[176] i.e. the meaning of these words is in the scriptures of Ibrāhīm and Mūsā.

وَكَانَ صُحُفُ إِبْرَاهِيْمَ أَقْرَبَ إِلَى الوَعْظِ. وَقِيْلَ: فِي صُحُفِ إِبْرَاهِيْمَ: «يَنْبَغِي لِلْعَاقِلِ أَنْ يَكُوْنَ حَافِظًا لِلِسَانِهِ، عَارِفًا بِزَمَانِهِ، مُقْبِلًا عَلَى شَأْنِهِ».

The scriptures of Ibrāhīm were closer to exhortations. It is said that within the scriptures of Ibrāhīm is [the following advice]: "The reasonable person must guard his tongue, know his time, and face his affairs."[177]

وَكَانَ الغَالِبُ عَلَى صُحُفِ مُوْسَى الأَحْكَامُ، أَمَّا المَوَاعِظُ فَقَلِيْلَةٌ. وَمِنْهَا الزَّوَاجِرُ البَلِيْغَةِ كَاللَّعْنِ لِمَنْ خَالَفَ أَوَامِرَ التَّوْرَاةِ الَّتِي أَعْظَمُهَا البِشَارَةِ بِمُحَمَّدٍ ﷺ.

The scriptures of Mūsā were predominantly legislation. They contained few exhortations, including severe rebukes, such as cursing whoever violates the commands of the Torah—the greatest one [of those commands] being the announcement of Muḥammad (may Allah bless him and give him peace).[178]

وَيَجِبُ مَعْرِفَةُ الكُتُبِ الأَرْبَعَةِ تَفْصِيْلًا، وَهِيَ:

It is obligatory to know four books specifically. They are:

---

176 Al-Aʿlā, 87:18–19.

177 Abū Nuʿaym al-Asfahānī, *Ḥilyat al-awliyā'* (Cairo: Al-Saʿādah, 1974/1394), 1:187; al-Bayhaqī, *Shuʿab al-īmān*, 6:373 #4353.

178 The contents of previous revelation are mentioned in many *tafsīrs*, including Al-Shirbīnī, *Al-Sirāj al-munīr*, 4:524.

التَّـوْرَاةُ المُنَزَّلَةُ جُمْلَةً عَلَى مُوْسَـى بْنِ عِمْـرانَ، وَيُعَبَّرُ عَنْهَا بِالعِبْرِيَّةِ، وَهِيَ لُغَةُ اليَهُوْدِ.

1 The Torah. It was revealed to Mūsā son of 'Imrān; it is formulated in Hebrew, the language of the Jews.

وَالإِنْجِيْلُ المُنَزَّلَةُ جُمْلَةً عَلَى عِيْسَى بْنِ(179) مَرْيَمَ، وَيُعبِّرُ عَنْهَا بالسُّرِيَانِيَّةِ.

2 The Injīl. It was revealed as a whole to 'Īsā son of Maryam; it is formulated in Syriac.

وَالزَّبُوْرُ المُنَزَّلَةُ عَلَى دَاوُدَ بْنِ إِيْشَا، وَيُعَبَّرُ عَنْهَا بِالسُّرِيَانِيَّةِ أَيْضًا.

3 The Zabūr. It was revealed to Dāwūd son of Īshā; it is also formulated in Syriac.

وَالقُرْآنُ المُنَزَّلُ مُنَجَّمًا فِي ثَلَاثَةٍ وَعِشْـرِيْنَ سَـنَةً بَعْدَ أَنْ أُنْزِلَ دُفْعَةً وَاحِدَةً فِي لَيْلَةِ القَدْرِ فِي بَيْتِ العِزَّةِ.

4 The Qur'ān. It was revealed in instalments during [a period of] twenty-three years, after being revealed all at once during the Night of Power [*Laylat al-qadr*] to the Mighty House [*bayt al-'izzah*].

وَيَجِبُ إِيْمَانُ الكُتُبِ(180) غَيْرِهَا إِجْمَالًا، كَمَا تَقَدَّمَ.

It is obligatory to believe in the other books overall, as has preceded.

179 A: «بـن». Perhaps «ابـن» would be better since the next name is not for the biological father of the prior. (And Allah knows best.)

180 This is as it is in the printed editions. Perhaps «...ويجـب الإيمـان بالكتـب غيرهـا», or «...ويجـب الإيمـان بغيرهـا مـن الكتـب» would be better. (And Allah knows best.)

THE LINEAGE OF THE PROPHET ﷺ [معرفة نسب النّبيّ المصطفى ﷺ]

وَيَجِبُ مَعْرِفَةُ نَسَبِ سَيِّدِنَا مُحَمَّدٍ ﷺ مِنْ جِهَةِ أَبِيهِ وَمِنْ جِهَةِ أُمِّهِ.

It is obligatory to know the lineage of our master Muḥammad ﷺ from his father's side and his mother's side.

فَأَمَّا نَسَبُهُ ﷺ مِنْ جِهَةِ أَبِيهِ، فَهُوَ: ابْنُ عَبْدِ اللَّهِ بْنِ عَبْدِ المُطَّلِبِ بْنِ هَاشِمِ بْنِ عَبْدِ مَنَافِ بْنِ قُصَيِّ بْنِ كِلَابِ بْنِ مُرَّةَ بْنِ كَعْبِ بْنِ لُؤَيِّ بْنِ غَالِبِ بْنِ فِهْرِ بْنِ مَالِكِ بْنِ النَّضْرِ بْنِ كِنَانَةَ بْنِ خُزَيْمَةَ بْنِ مُدْرِكَةَ بْنِ إِلْيَاسَ بْنِ مُضَرِ بْنِ نِزَارِ بْنِ مَعَدِّ بْنِ عَدْنَانَ.

As for his lineage from his father's side, he ﷺ is:

- [Muḥammad] son of
- 'Abd Allāh son of
- 'Abd al-Muṭṭalib son of
- Hāshim son of
- 'Abd Manāf son of
- Quṣayy son of
- Kilāb son of
- Murrah son of
- Ka'b son of
- Lu'ayy son of
- Ghālib son of
- Fihr son of
- Mālik son of
- al-Naḍar son of
- Kinānah son of
- Khuzaymah son of
- Mudrikah son of
- Ilyās son of

- Muḍar son of
- Nizār son of
- Ma'add son of
- 'Adnān.

فَلَا تَجِبُ مَعْرِفَةُ مَا بَعْدَ عَدْنَانَ بِلَا خِلَافٍ، بَلْ كَرِهَهُ الإِمَامُ مَالِكٌ.

It is not obligatory to know what comes after 'Adnān, without any disagreement. Indeed, Imām Mālik disliked it.

وَأَمَّا نَسَبُهُ مِنْ جِهَةِ أُمِّهِ فَهِيَ: آمِنَةُ بِنْتُ وَهْبِ بْنِ عَبْدِ مَنَافِ بْنِ زُهْرَةَ بْنِ كِلَابِ بْنِ مُرَّةَ إِلَى عَدْنَانَ أَيْضًا.

As for his lineage from his mother's side, she is

- Āminah daughter of
- Wahb son of
- 'Abd Manāf son of
- Zuhrah son of
- Kilāb son of
- Murrah upto 'Adnān also.

فَتَجْتَمِعُ أُمُّهُ مَعَهُ ﷺ فِي جِهَةِ جَدِّهِ كِلَابٍ.

His mother meets his father (May Allah bless him and give him peace) [i.e. they share the same lineage] from the direction of his grandfather Kilāb.

HIS NOBLE APPEARANCE ﷺ — [مَعرِفَةُ وَصْفِهِ الشَّرِيْفِ ﷺ]

يَجِبُ مَعْرِفَةُ لَوْنِهِ ﷺ؛ فَإِنَّهُ أَبْيَضُ مُشْـرَبٌ بِحُمْرَةٍ(181)، سَـالِمٌ مِنْ الدَّنَسِ ظَاهِرًا وَبَاطِنًا.

It is obligatory to know his complexion ﷺ: he was relatively light in colour blended with red, free from any outward or internal blemish.

HIS CHILDREN عليهم السلام — [مَعرِفَةُ ساداتِنا أَولادِهِ عليهم السلام]

(٢٩) وَأَوْلَادُهُ(182) قَاسِمْ وَزَيْنَبٌ أَتَتْ * رُقَيَّـةٌ وَفَاطِمَـةْ قَـدِ احْتَـذَتْ

(29) And [his] children Qāsim, and Zaynab arrived * Ruqayyah, and Fāṭimah she followed

---

181 One of the basic rules when working with texts is that the uncertain and ambiguous words are interpreted in light of the certain and clear. While there are questions concerning the actual colour of his skin ﷺ, there is absolutely no question that prophets are free of any form of repulsive sickness or trait, and that the Prophet ﷺ was an Arab. Any physical description must be understood within the confines of what we are certain of. I have translated "*abyaḍ*" as "relatively light in colour" instead of "white" since the rest of the sentence, other narrations, and all of their commentaries clarify that the plain colour "white" is not what is intended, and mentioning it—even with its qualifiers—presents a disruptive distraction for some. The colours mentioned in the text are affirmatively mentioned in a narration in al-Tirmidhī (3683). Other narrations negate a few other colours, including being pale white [*al-abyaḍ al-amhaq*], or very swarthy [*al-adam*], as in Al-Bukhārī (5900) and Muslim (2347 #113). Ibn Taymiyyah stated that "his colour was white, wheat coloured" (*Kitāb al-masā'il wa-l-ajwibah*, 1:244). Imam al-Dhahabī wrote that, "When Arabs say someone is white, it means they are wheat coloured with a black fringe" (*Siyar a'lām al-nubalā'*, 2:168). However, their explanation does not appear to have been repeated until the 20th century. (And Allah knows best.)

182 This is as all editions have it, though starting with «أولادُهُ» would be better for the metre.

(٣٠) وَأُمُّ كَلْثُومٍ وَعَبْدُ اللهِ ثُمَّ * إِبْرَاهِيمٌ مِنْ مَارِيَهْ فَادْرِ وَرُمْ

(30) Umm Kalthūm, and ʿAbd Allāh then * Ibrāhīm from Māriyah so be cognisant of them

أَي: يَنْبَغِي لِكُلِّ شَخْصٍ مَعْرِفَةُ أَوْلَادِهِ ﷺ لِأَنَّهُمْ سَادَةُ الأُمَّةِ؛ فَيَنْبَغِي لَهُ أَنْ يَعْرِفَ سَادَتَهُ، وَهُمْ سَبْعَةٌ.

Everyone should know his children ﷺ since they are the community's nobility, and one should know his nobles. They are seven.

الأَوَّلُ: قَاسِمٌ، فَهُوَ أَوَّلُ وَلَدِهِ ﷺ وَبِهِ كَانَ ﷺ يُكَنَّى. وَعَاشَ حَتَّى مَشَى، وَهُوَ أَوَّلُ مَنْ مَاتَ مِنْ وَلَدِهِ ﷺ.

1 Qāsim. His first child ﷺ, and the source of his [the Prophet's] patronym ["Abū Qāsim"] ﷺ. He lived long enough to walk. He is the first of his children to die ﷺ.

وَالثَّانِي: زَيْنَبُ، فَهِيَ أَكْبَرُ بَنَاتِهِ، مَاتَتْ أَوَّلَ سَنَةِ ثَمَانٍ مِنَ الهِجْرَةِ عِنْدَ زَوْجِهَا لَقِيطِ بْنِ هَالَةَ بِنْتِ خُوَيْلِدٍ. وَلَدَتْ لَهُ عَلِيًّا وَأُمَامَةَ الَّتِي حَمَلَهَا رَسُوْلُ اللهِ ﷺ فِي صَلَاةِ الصُّبْحِ عَلَى عَاتِقِهِ.

2 Zaynab. His eldest daughter. She died at the beginning of 8 AH while married to Laqīṭ bin Hālah bint Khuwaylid. She bore him ʿAlī and Umāmah. The Messenger of Allah ﷺ carried her [Umāmah] on his shoulders during morning prayer.

وَالثَّالِثُ: رُقَيَّةُ، وَكَانَتْ تَحْتَ عُتْبَةَ بْنِ أَبِي لَهَبٍ، وَكَانَ عُتْبَةُ -بِالتَّكْبِيرِ- أَسْلَمَ فِي الفَتْحِ ثُمَّ بَعْدَ المُفَارَقَةِ تَزَوَّجَهَا عُثْمَانُ بْنُ عَفَّانَ بِمَكَّةَ. وَكَانَتْ بَارِعَةَ الجَمَالِ، وَكَانَ عُثْمَانُ جَمِيلًا. وَتُوُفِّيَتْ وَالنَّبِيُّ ﷺ بِبَدْرٍ وَهِيَ ابْنَةُ عِشْرِيْنَ سَنَةً.

3 Ruqayyah. She was married to ʿUtbah bin Abī Lahab. He entered Islam when Mecca was conquered. After separation [from ʿUtbah], ʿUthmān bin ʿAffān married her in Mecca. She was extremely beautiful and ʿUthmān was handsome. She passed away while the Prophetﷺ was at Badr; she was twenty years old.

وَالرَّابِعُ: فَاطِمَةُ الزَّهْرَاءُ، وَتَزَوَّجَتْ بِعَلِيِّ بْنِ أَبِي طَالِبٍ، وَلَهَا خَمْسَ عَشْرَةَ سَنَةً وَخَمْسَةُ أَشْهُرٍ وَنِصْفٌ، وَلِعَلِيٍّ إِحْدَى وَعِشْرُوْنَ سَنَةً وَخَمْسَةُ أَشْهُرٍ. وَوَلَدَتْ حَسَنًا، وَحُسَيْنًا، وَمُحَسِّنًا -بِضَمِّ الْمِيمِ وَفَتْحِ الْحَاءِ الْمُهْمَلَةِ وَكَسْرِ السِّيْنِ الْمُشَدَّدَةِ-، وَأُمَّ كَلْثُومٍ، وَزَيْنَبَ.

4 Fāṭimāh al-Zahrāʾ. At the age of fifteen years and five and a half months, she married ʿAlī bin Abī Ṭālib; he was twenty-one years and five months old. She gave birth to Ḥasan, Ḥusayn, Muḥassin (with a *ḍammah* on the *mīm*, *fatḥah* on the undottet *ḥāʾ*, and a *kasrah* under the doubled *sīn*), Umm Kalthūm, and Zaynab.

وَقَوْلُهُ: ((قَدْ احْتَذَتْ))، أَيْ: قَدْ تَبِعَتْ فَاطِمَةُ مَنْ تَقَدَّمَ فِي الذِّكْرِ.

Him [the versifier] saying, "she followed [*qad iḥtadhat*]," i.e. Fāṭimah came after the ones who were mentioned earlier.

وَالْخَامِسُ: أُمُّ كَلْثُومٍ، وَاسْمُهَا كُنْيَتُهَا، وَقِيْلَ: اسْمُهَا زَيْنَبُ الصُّغْرَى. وَكَانَتْ عِنْدَ عُتَيْبَةَ بْنِ أَبِي لَهَبٍ، وَعُتَيْبَةُ -بِالتَّصْغِيْرِ- مَاتَ كَافِرًا. وَقَدْ تَزَوَّجَ بِهَا عُثْمَانُ بْنُ عَفَّانَ بَعْدَ مَوْتِ أُخْتِهَا رُقَيَّةَ، وَرُوِيَ أَنَّهُ ﷺ قَالَ لَهُ: ((وَالَّذِي نَفْسِي بِيَدِهِ، لَوْ أَنَّ عِنْدِي مِائَةَ بِنْتٍ يَمُتْنَ وَاحِدَةً بَعْدَ وَاحِدَةٍ زَوَّجْتُكَ أُخْرَى بَعْدَ أُخْرَى)).

5 Umm Kalthūm. Her name is her eponym [i.e. "Umm Kalthūm"]. Another opinion is that her name is "Zaynab the Younger." She

was married to 'Utaybah bin Abī Lahab who died a disbeliever. Afterwards, 'Uthmān bin 'Affān married her after her sister Ruqayyah had died. It was reported that he ﷺ said, "If I had one hundred daughters, each one dying after the other, I would have married them to you one after the other."[183]

وَالسَّادِسُ: عَبْدُ اللَّهِ، مَاتَ صَغِيْرًا بِمَكَّةَ، وَيُلَقَّبُ بِـ«الطَّيِّبِ» وَ«الطَّاهِرِ» عَلَى الصَّحِيْحِ؛ لِأَنَّهُ وُلِدَ بَعْدَ النُّبُوَّةِ.

6 'Abd Allāh. He died at an early age in Mecca. He is nicknamed "the wholesome [*al-ṭayyib*]" and "the pure [*al-ṭāhir*]" (according to the sound opinion), since he was born after the prophecy [began].

وَهَؤُلَاءِ السِّتَّةُ مِنْ خَدِيْجَةَ.

Those six [children] are with Khadījah.

وَالسَّابِعُ: إِبْرَاهِيْمُ، وَهُوَ آخِرُ أَوْلَادِهِ ﷺ، وَهُوَ مِنْ مَارِيَةَ القِبْطِيَّةِ.

7 Ibrāhīm. He is the last of his children ﷺ. He was from Māriyah the Copt.

MATTERS EXCLUSIVE TO THE PROPHET ﷺ

[مَعرِفَةُ خَصائِصِ النَّبيِّ ﷺ]

(٣١) وَاعْرِفْ خَصَائِصَ النَّبِيْ مِنْ وَاجِبَهْ * مُـحَـرَّمٍ تَـخْـفِـيْـفَـةٍ فَـضِـيْـلَـةْ

(31) The best known matters exclusive to the Prophet are obligatory, * unlawful, lightened, or a superior quality

---

183 Ibn 'Asākir, *Tārīkh Dimashq* (Beirut: Dār al-Fikr, 1995/1415), 39:39; al-Suyūṭī, *Jam' al-jawāmi'*, 24531/170.

قَالَ النَّوَوِيُّ: «وَلَا يَبْعُدُ القَوْلُ بِوُجُوبِ ذِكْرِ خَصَائِصِهِ ﷺ لِئَلَّا يَرَى الجَاهِلُ بَعْضَ الخَصَائِصِ فِي الخَبَرِ الصَّحِيْحِ فَيَعْمَلَ بِهِ أَخْذًا بِأَصْلِ التَّأَسِّي، فَوَجَبَ بَيَانُهَا لِتُعْرَفَ.

Al-Nawawī said: "The opinion that it is obligatory to mention which matters are exclusive to the Prophet ﷺ is not unreasonable lest the ignorant see some exclusive matters in authentic reports and act upon them according to the principle of following his example. Accordingly, it is obligatory to clarify them."[184]

وَهِيَ أَرْبَعَةُ أَنْوَاعٍ.

There are four types [of exclusive matters].[185]

أَحَدُهَا: الواجِبَاتُ، وَهِيَ أَشْيَاءُ كَثِيْرَةٌ، مِنْهَا: الضُّحَى، وَالوِتْرُ، وَالأُضْحِيَّةُ.

1 Obligatory Acts. There are many, including
- Praying the Mid-morning [Ḍuḥā] and Witr Prayers.
- Slaughtering for Eid al-Aḍḥā.

وَمِنْهَا: السِّوَاكُ لِكُلِّ صَلَاةٍ، وَالمُشَاوَرَةُ لِذَوِي الأَحْلَامِ فِي الأَمْرِ، وَتَخْيِيْرُ نِسَائِهِ بَيْنَ مُفَارَقَتِهِ طَلَبًا لِلدُّنْيَا وَاخْتِيَارِهِ طَلَبًا لِلآخِرَةِ.

They include
- Using *miswāk* with every prayer.
- Seeking advice from notables in matters.
- Giving his wives the option between leaving him in order to seek this world, and choosing him out of seeking the afterlife.

184 al-Nawawī, *Rawḍat al-ṭalibīn* (Beirut: Al-Maktab al-Islāmī, 1991/1412), 7:17–18.

185 Shafiʿīs often mentioned these matters at the beginning of the chapter on marriage. I included many of them—along with their evidence—in *The Evident Memorandum*. See also al-Nawawī, *Rawḍat al-ṭālibīn*, 6:3–11; al-Anṣārī, *Asnā al-maṭālib* (Beirut: Al-Maktab al-Islāmī, n.d.), 3:98–103.

وَالثَّانِـي: المُحَرَّمَاتُ، وَهِيَ أَشْـيَاءُ كَثِيْرَةٌ، مِنْهَا: الـزَّكَاةُ وَالصَّدَقَةُ، وَتَعَلُّمُ الخَـطِّ، وَالشِّـعْرُ، وَمَدُّ العَيْنِ إِلَى مَتَاعِ الدُّنْيَـا، وَخَائِنَةُ الأَعْيُنِ -وَهِيَ[186] الإِيْمَاءُ بِمَا يُظْهِرُ خِلَافَهُ- دُوْنَ الخَدِيْعَةِ فِي الحَرْبِ، وَإِمْسَاكُ مَنْ كَرِهَتْ نِكَاحَهُ.

وَمِنْهَا: نِكَاحُ كِتَابِيَّةٍ لَا لِلتَّسَرِّي بِهَا.

2 Unlawful Acts. They are many, including
- [Accepting] zakat and charity.
- Learning to write and composing poetry.
- Extending his gaze to the luxuries of this life.
- Deception (which is hinting that something is other than what it seems)—though not tricks during warfare.
- Keeping a woman who dislikes him as a wife.

They also include
- Marrying a woman from the people of the book (though not sleeping with her as a lawful slave).

الثَّالِثُ: التَّخْفِيْفَاتُ وَالمُبَاحَاتُ، وَهِيَ كَثِيْرَةٌ جِدًّا.

3 Lightened or Permissible Acts. They are very numerous.

مِنْهَا: تَزْوِيْجُ مَنْ شَـاءَ لِمَنْ شَـاءَ -وَلَوْ لِنَفْسِـهِ- بِغَيْرِ إِذْنٍ مِنَ المَرْأَةِ وَوَلِيِّهَا مُتَوَلِّيًا لِلطَّرَفَيْنِ.

They include
- Marrying whomever he wishes to whomever he wishes (even to himself) without permission from the woman and her guardian, while fulfilling both sides of the contract [i.e. the offer and acceptance].

---

186 Ustaz Zainul Abidin mentioned that A has «وهـو», and perhaps what is mentioned here is better.

وَأُبِيْحَ لَهُ الوِصَالُ، وَصَفِيُّ المَغْنَمِ، وَيَحْكُمُ وَيَشْهَدُ لِوَلَدِهِ وَلَوْ لِنَفْسِهِ.

It was permissible for him to

- Fast uninterruptedly.
- Pick from the spoils of war [before its distribution].
- Judge a case and offer testimony on behalf of his child (and even for himself).

وَأُبِيْحَ لَهُ نِكَاحُ تِسْعٍ. وَقَدْ تَزَوَّجَ ﷺ بِضْعَ عَشَرَةٍ، وَمَاتَ عَنْ تِسْعٍ. وَيَنْعَقِدُ نِكَاحُهُ مُحْرِمًا بِالنُّسُكِ وَبِلَفْظِ الهِبَةِ لَا قَبُوْلًا، وَلَا مَهْرَ لِلوَاهِبَةِ لَهُ وَإِنْ دَخَلَ بِهَا. وَتَجِبُ إِجَابَتُهُ عَلَى امْرَأَةٍ رَغِبَ فِيْهَا، وَيَجِبُ عَلَى زَوْجِهَا طَلَاقُهَا لِيَنْكِحَهَا.

It was permitted for him to

- Marry nine women. He ﷺ married just over ten [in total]. He passed away while married to nine.

  It was valid and effective for him to:

- Marry while performing pilgrimage.
- [Marry] using the phrase of gifting to offer (but not to accept).
- [Marry] without a *mahr* [bridal gift] if a woman gifted herself to him; [it can remain *mahr*less] even if he did consummate the marriage.

  [Also]

- If the Prophet was interested in marrying a woman who was married, it would be obligatory upon the husband to divorce her so he could marry her.

الرَّابِعُ: الفَضَائِلُ، وَهِيَ كَثِيْرَةٌ لَا تَدْخُلُ تَحْتَ الحَصْرِ، مِنْهَا: تَحْرِيْمُ مَنْكُوْحَاتِهِ مُطْلَقًا عَلَى غَيْرِهِ، وَتَحْرِيْمُ إِمَائِهِ المَوْطُوْءَةِ مِنْهَا.

4 Merits. They are numerous and cannot be counted, including

- The unlawfulness of anyone else marrying any of his wives

(without restriction [i.e. even if they were divorced, and even if the marriage was not consummated]).

- The impermissibility of any slave women with whom he had intercourse.

وَمِنْهَا: أَنَّهُ أَوَّلُ مَنْ يَقْرَعُ بَابَ الجَنَّةِ، وَأَوَّلُ شَافِعٍ، وَأَوَّلُ مُشَفَّعٍ، وَأُكْرِمَ بِالشَّفَاعَاتِ الخَمْسِ يَوْمَ القِيَامَةِ.

They include that he is

- The first who will knock on the door of Paradise.
- The first who will intercede and the first whose intercession is accepted.

He is blessed with five intercessions on the Day of Resurrection. [They are:]

أُوْلَاهَا: العُظْمَى، فِي الفَصْلِ بَيْنَ أَهْلِ المَوْقِفِ حِينَ يَفْزَعُوْنَ إِلَيْهِ بَعْدَ الأَنْبِيَاءِ.

1. The grand intercession of separating [disputes] between the people waiting for judgment when they flee to him ﷺ after the Prophets.

الثَّانِيَةُ: فِي إِدْخَالِ خَلْقٍ الجَنَّةَ بِغَيْرِ حِسَابٍ -جَعَلَنَا اللَّهُ وَأَحْبَابَنَا مِنْهُمْ.

2. [Interceding for] people to enter Paradise without being judged (may Allah make us and our loved ones among them!).

الثَّالِثُ: فِي نَاسٍ اسْتَحَقُّوْا دُخُوْلَ النَّارِ فَلَا يَدْخُلُوْنَهَا.

3. [Interceding so that] people deserving of entering the hellfire do not enter it.

الرَّابِعُ: فِي نَاسٍ دَخَلُوْا النَّارَ فَيُخْرَجُوْنَ مِنْهَا.

4. [Interceding] for people who entered the hellfire to be removed from it.

الخَامِسَةُ[187]: فِي رَفْعِ دَرَجَاتِ نَاسٍ فِي الجَنَّةِ.

5. [Interceding to] raise peoples' ranks in Paradise.

وَخُصَّ ﷺ مِنْهَا بِالعُظْمَى وَدُخُوْلِ خَلْقٍ مِنْ أُمَّتِهِ الجَنَّةَ بِغَيْرِ حِسَابٍ، وَنَصَرَ ﷺ بِالرُّعْبِ مَسِيْرَةَ شَهْرٍ، وَجُعِلَتْ الأَرْضُ مَسْجَدًا وَتُرَابُهَا طَهُوْرًا، وَأُحِلَّتْ لَهُ الغَنَائِمُ، وَأُرْسِلَ إِلَى الكَافَّةِ وَرِسَالَةُ غَيْرِهِ خَاصَّةٌ، وَهُوَ أَكْثَرُ الأَنْبِيَاءِ أَتْبَاعًا. وَأُمَّتُهُ خَيْرُ الأُمَمِ وَأَفْضَلُهَا أَصْحَابُهُ وَأَفْضَلُهُمْ الخُلَفَاءُ الأَرْبَعَةِ عَلَى تَرْتِيْبِهِمْ فِي الخِلَافَةِ ثُمَّ بَاقِي العَشَرَةِ.

He ﷺ was singled out with

- The grand intercession.
- Part of his community entering Paradise without [first] being judged.
- Him ﷺ being supported through fear [being struck into the hearts of his opponents] for a distance of one month's travel.
- The ground being a place to pray and its earth a means of purification.
- Spoils of war being licit to him.
- Being sent as a messenger to everyone while the message of others [i.e. previous prophets] was restricted.
- He is the prophet with the largest number of followers.
- His community is the best community of all.

---

187 Ustaz Zainul Abidin mentioned that A has «الخامس», and perhaps what is mentioned here is better.

The best of his community are his Companions,[188] with the best of them being the four Caliphs in order of their caliphate,[189] then the rest of the ten [who were promised Paradise].[190]

وَهِـيَ مَعْصُومَـةٌ لَا تَجْتَمِـعُ عَلَـى ضَلَالَةٍ. ولَهَا فَضَائِلُ كَثِيْرَةٌ عَلَى سَـائِرِ الأُمَمِ، مِنْهَا: أَنَّهَا أَوَّلُ مَنْ يَدْخُلُ الجَنَّةَ بَعْدَ الأَنْبِيَاءِ عليهم السلام. وَمِنْهَا: وَضْعُ الإِصْرِ، وَلَيْلَةُ القَدْرِ، وَالجُمُعَةُ، وَرَمَضَانُ عَلَى أَحَدِ قَوْلَيْنِ.

- [His community] is protected: it will not unanimously agree upon a misguidance
- His community has numerous qualities which are superior to all other communities. They include
    - It being the first to enter Paradise after the prophets ﷺ.
    - The removal of the heavy burden [alluded to in Q2:286].
    - The Night of Power, the day of Friday, and the month of Ramadan (according to one of two opinions).[191]

188 *Jawharah*, 75; *Tuḥfah*, 485.

189 Abū Bakr al-Ṣiḍḍīq, ʿUmar bin al-Khaṭṭāb, ʿUthmān bin ʿAffān, and ʿAlī bin Abī Ṭālib (may Allah be pleased with them all). *Jawharah*, 76; *Tuḥfah*, 491, 493.

190 Ṭalḥah bin ʿUbaydallāh, al-Zubayr bin al-ʿAwwām, ʿAbd al-Raḥmān bin ʿAwf, Saʿd bin Abī Waqqāṣ, Saʿīd bin Zayd, and Abū ʿUbaydah ʿĀmir bin al-Jarrāḥ. *Jawharah*, 77; *Tuḥfah*, 495–96. See al-Tirmidhī, 3747.

They are then followed by those who participated in Badr, Uḥud, Bayʿat Riḍwān, and the earliest to accept Islam. *Jawharah*, 78–79; *Tuḥfah*, 497–504.

191 This entire section on matters exclusive to the Prophet ﷺ, with minor differences, matches what is in al-Shirbīnī's *Al-Sirāj al-munīr*, 3:259–261.

ESSENTIALS FOR UPHOLDING THE RELIGION

[مَعرِفَةُ ما لا بُدَّ مِنهُ في إقامَةِ الدّينِ]

(٣٢) وَلِإِقَــامِ الـدِّيْـنِ كَـالـطَّـهَـارَةِ * وَالـصَّـوْمِ وَالـصَّـلَاةِ وَالـزَّكَـاةِ

(32) And [knowing what is obligatory] to uphold the religion, like purification * And fasting, and prayer, and zakat

أَي: يَجِبُ مَعْرِفَةُ مَا لَا بُدَّ مِنْهُ فِي إِقَامَةِ مَفْرُوْضَاتِ الدِّيْنِ. وَيَكْفِي فِي ذَلِكَ مَعْرِفَةُ أَحْكَامِها الظَّاهِرَةِ، نَحْوُ كَلِمَتَي الشَّهَادَةِ مَعَ فَهْمِ مَعْنَاهُمَا بِحَيْثُ يَجْزِمُ اعْتِقادَهُ بِذَلِكَ، وَقَدْ تَقَدَّمَ هَذَا أَوَّلًا.

It is obligatory to know whatever is needed to uphold [and maintain] the obligatory acts of religion. It suffices to know their outward rulings, such as

- The two phrases of the testification of faith [*shahādah*], and understanding their meaning in order that one is convinced in his belief in it. (This is preceded in the beginning [of the book].)

وَنَحْوُ وَاجِبَاتِ الطَّهَارَةِ مِنْ وُضُوْءٍ وَغُسْلٍ وَتَيَمُّمٍ وَإِزَالَةِ النَّجَاسَةِ،

- Duties related to the various forms of purification (including ablution, the purificatory bath, dry ablution, removing filth).

وَنَحْوُ الصَّلَاةِ وَالصَّوْمِ،

- Prayer and fasting.

وَنَحْوُ وَاجِبَاتِ مَا لَزِمَهُ مِنَ الزَّكَاةِ،

- The duties related to whatever zakat is required of him.

وَنَحْوُ كَيْفِيَّةِ الحَجِّ إِذَا عَزَمَ عَلَيْهِ،

- How to perform Hajj if he decides to perform it.

وَنَحْوُ مَا تَتَوَقَّفُ عَلَيْهِ صِحَّةُ النَّوَافِلِ وَالمُعَامَلاتِ إِذَا أَرَادَ فِعْلَهَا

- Whatever voluntary acts and transactions require in order to be valid, should he choose to perform them.

C. OBLIGATORY AS ACTIONS [قِسمُ ما يَجِبُ وُجوبَ عَمَلٍ]

ثُمَّ شَرَعَ النَّاظِمُ فِي القِسْمِ الثَّالِثِ مِنْ الأَقْسَامِ التَّابِعَةِ، وَهُوَ مَا يَجِبُ وُجُوْبَ العَمَلِ، فَقَالَ:

The versifier then began the third supplement, which is what is obligatory as actions. He said:

(٣٣) وَاعْمَلْ بِتَقْلِيْدِ إِمَامٍ ثُمَّا * حِفْظٍ لِكُلِّيَّاتٍ ثُمَّ تَمِّمَا

(33) **Act by emulating an Imām then * Preserving the universal [obligations], then finish up**

(٣٤) بِتَرْكِ تَسْمِيعٍ وَعُجْبٍ كِبْرٍ * رِيَا حَسَدٍ[192] اغْتِيَابِ غَيْرِ

(34) **By ceasing from telling of one's works, and pride, arrogance, * Showing off, envy, backbiting, talebearing others**

EMULATING QUALIFIED SCHOLARSHIP [وُجُوبُ تَقليدِ الأَئِمَّةِ المُجتَهِدينَ]

أَي: يَجِبُ عَلَى مَنْ لَمْ يَكُنْ فِي أَهْلِيَّةِ الاجْتِهَادِ المُطْلَقِ تَقْلِيْدُ مُجْتَهِدٍ مُطْلَقٍ فِي الفُرُوْعِ مِنْ أَحَدِ الأَئِمَةِ المَشْهُوْرِيْنَ: الإِمَامِ الشَّافِعِيِّ، وَالإِمَامِ أَبِي حَنِيْفَةَ، وَالإِمَامِ مَالِكٍ، وَالإِمَامِ أَحْمَدَ بْنِ حَنْبَلٍ رضي الله عنهم.

Meaning: It is obligatory for someone who is not qualified to perform absolute *ijtihād* to emulate an imam who is an absolute *mujtahid* in derived issues,[193] including one of the famous Imams [i.e.] Imam

192 A adds «نَمِيمَةٍ» after this. Unfortunately, its inclusion breaks the metre.
193 *Jawharah*, 82; *Tuḥfah*, 524.

al-Shāfiʿī, Imam Abū Ḥanīfah, Imam Mālik, and Imam Aḥmad ﷺ.[194]

وَاخْتِلَافُ العُلَمَاءِ رَحْمَةٌ.

Variance [in legal issues] between the scholars is a mercy.[195]

وَأَخْذُ قَوْلِ المُجْتَهِدِ وَاجِبٌ مِنْ حَيْثُ أَنَّهُ أَدَّاهُ اجْتِهَادُهُ إِلَى أَنَّهُ حَقٌّ وَإِنْ لَمْ يُطَابِقْ الوَاقِعَ. «وَمَا يَقُوْلُ مُجْتَهِدٌ قَوْلًا إِلَّا قَالَ بِهِ أَصْحَابِي».

Taking the opinion of a *mujtahid* is obligatory in that his *ijtihād* brought him to consider it correct even if it is not actually so in reality. "And no mujtahid issues an opinion save that my Companions said it."[196]

وَقَدْ وَرَدَ أَنَّ رَجُلًا حَلَفَ أَنَّهُ لَا يَطَأُ زَوْجَتَهُ حِيْنًا، فَأَفْتَاهُ أَبُو بَكْرٍ بِأَنَّ الحِيْنَ الأَبَدُ، وَأَفْتَاهُ عُمَرُ أَنَّهُ أَرْبَعُوْنَ سَنَةً، وَأَفْتَاهُ عُثْمَانُ بِأَنَّهُ سَنَةٌ وَاحِدَةٌ(197)، وَأَفْتَاهُ عَلِيٌّ بِأَنَّهُ يَوْمٌ وَاحِدٌ وَلَيْلَةٌ.

فَعَرَضَ الرَّجُلُ ذَلِكَ عَلَى رَسُوْلِ اللهِ ﷺ فَدَعَا بِهِمْ، فَقَالَ لِأَبِي بَكْرٍ: «مَا دَلِيْلُكَ عَلَى أَنَّ الحِيْنَ الأَبَدُ؟»

قَالَ: دَلِيْلِي قَوْلُهُ تَعَالَى فِي حَقِّ قَوْمِ [يُوْنُسَ(198)] ﴿فَمَتَّعْنَاهُمْ إِلَى حِيْنٍ﴾، أَي: أَبْقَيْنَاهُم مُمَتِّعِيْنَ بِمَا لَهُمْ إِلَى انْقِضَاءِ أَعْمَارِهِمْ.

194 *Jawharah*, 81, 82; *Tuḥfah*, 514–15, 524.

195 The earliest mention of this statement is Abū ʿAbd al-Raḥmān al-Sulamī's *Ṭabaqāt al-ṣūfiyyah* (Beirut: Dār al-Kutub al-ʿIlmiyyah, 1997/1419), where he attributed it to Abū Yazīd [al-Busṭāmī]. It is clear in that passage that this mercy excludes differences in matters related to creed. (And Allah knows best.)

196 Translated as it appears in the original. I was not able to find a source for this statement.

197 Ustaz Zainul Abidin mentioned that A has «واحد», and perhaps what is mentioned here is better.

198 A: «نوح», and perhaps «يونس» is better.

وَقَالَ لِعُمَرَ: «مَا دَلِيْلُكَ عَلَى أَنَّ الحِيْنَ أَرْبَعُوْنَ سَنَةً؟»

قَالَ: دَلِيْلِي قَوْلُهُ تَعَالَى: ﴿هَلْ أَتَىٰ عَلَى الإِنْسَانِ حِيْنٌ مِّنَ الدَّهْرِ﴾، فَالإِنْسَانُ آدَمُ: أُلْقِيَتْ طِيْنَتُهُ عَلَى بَابِ الجَنَّةِ أَرْبَعِيْنَ عَامًا وَأَمْطَرَ اللَّهُ عَلَيْهِ هُمُوْمًا وَأَحْزَانًا طُوْلَ هَذِهِ المُدَّةِ، وَأَمْطَرَ عَلَيْهِ سُرُوْرًا نِصْفَ يَوْمٍ، فَجَاءَتْ ذُرِّيَّتُهُ عَلَى ذَلِكَ.

وَقَالَ لِعُثْمَانَ: «مَا دَلِيْلُكَ عَلَى أَنَّ الحِيْنَ عَامٌ؟»

قَالَ: دَلِيْلِي قَوْلُهُ تَعَالَى: ﴿تُؤْتِي أُكُلَهَا كُلَّ حِيْنٍ﴾، أَي: تُعْطِي النَّخْلَةُ ثَمَرَتَهَا كُلَّ عَامٍ.

وَقَالَ لِعَلِيٍّ: «مَا دَلِيْلُكَ عَلَى أَنَّ الحِيْنَ يَوْمٌ وَلَيْلَةٌ؟»

قَالَ: دَلِيْلِي قَوْلُهُ تَعَالَى: ﴿فَسُبْحَانَ اللَّهِ حِيْنَ تُمْسُوْنَ وَحِيْنَ تُصْبِحُوْنَ﴾، أَي: سَبِّحُوْا اللهَ تَعَالَى حِيْنَ تَدْخُلُوْنَ فِي المَسَاءِ وَحِيْنَ تَدْخُلُوْنَ فِي الصَّبَاحِ؛ بِمَعْنَى: صَلُّوْا فِي وَقْتِ المَسَاءِ صَلَاةَ الظُّهْرِ وَالعَصْرِ وَالمَغْرِبِ وَالعِشَاءِ، وَفِي وَقْتِ الصَّبَاحِ صَلَاةَ الصُّبْحِ.

فَقَالَ ﷺ: «أَصْحَابِي كَالنُّجُوْمِ بِأَيِّهِمْ اقْتَدَيْتُمْ اهْتَدَيْتُمْ».

وَأَمَرَ ﷺ الرَّجُلَ أَنْ يَأْخُذَ قَوْلَ عَلِيٍّ تَخْفِيْفًا عَلَيْهِ.

وَقَالَ أَيْضًا: «أَقْضَاكُمْ عَلِيٌّ».

It was transmitted that

> A man swore that he would not have intercourse with his wife for a period of time [*ḥīn min al-dahr*]. [He sought legal opinions from Abū Bakr, 'Umar, 'Uthmān, and 'Alī (may Allah be pleased with them all) concerning the specific

duration of "a period of time."] Abū Bakr informed him the duration is forever; 'Umar informed him that it is forty years; 'Uthmān, that it is one year; and 'Alī, that it is a single day and night.

The man presented these [opinions] to the Messenger of Allah ﷺ, so he [ﷺ] called for them.

He [ﷺ] said to Abū Bakr, "What is your evidence that the duration is forever?"

He [Abū Bakr] replied, "My evidence is Him (Most High is He) saying concerning Yūnus's people 'so We allowed them comfort for a while [*ḥīn*],'[199] meaning: We let them remain comforted with their possessions for the rest of their lives."

He [ﷺ] said to 'Umar, "What is your evidence that the duration is forty years?"

He ['Umar] said, "My evidence is Him (Most High is He) saying, 'Has there [not] come upon man a period of time [*ḥīn min al-dahr*] when he was not a thing [even] mentioned?'[200] The man [in the verse] is Ādam. His clay was put on the door of Paradise for forty years; Allah rained anxieties and sorrows upon it that entire time, and rained happinesses upon it for half a day. And this is how his descendants are."

He [ﷺ] said to 'Uthmān, "What is your evidence that the duration is one year?"

---

199 Al-Ṣaffāt, 37:148.
200 Al-Insān, 76:1.

He ['Uthmān] replied, "My evidence is Him Most High saying, 'It produces its fruit every season [*kulla ḥīn*],'[201] meaning: the date gives its fruit every year."

He [ﷺ] said to 'Alī, "What is your evidence that the duration is a single day and night?"

He ['Alī] replied, "My evidence is Him (Most High is He) saying, 'So exalt Allah in [*ḥīn*] the evening and in the morning,'[202] meaning: exalt Allah (Most High is He) when you enter the evening and when you enter the morning, meaning: During the evening time, pray the noon-prayer, the mid-afternoon prayer, the sunset prayer, and the night prayer; and pray the morning prayer during the morning time."

He ﷺ then said, "My Companions are like stars: whichever one you follow, you will be guided."[203] He ﷺ commanded the man to take the opinion of 'Alī to make things easier for him. He [may Allah bless him peace] also said, "The best of you in deciding cases is 'Alī."[204]

وَمَذْهَبُ الشّافِعِيِّ حَمْلُ «الحِيْنِ» عَلَى مُضِيِّ لَحْظَةٍ مِنْ الزَّمَانِ، وَمَذْهَبُ مَالِكٍ مِثْلُ قَوْلِ عُثْمَانَ، وَمَذْهَبُ أَبِي حَنِيْفَةَ وَأَحْمَدَ حَمْلُ الحِيْنِ عَلَى

201 Ibrāhīm, 14:25.

202 Al-Rūm, 30:17.

203 Ibn Mulaqqin, *Tadhkirat al-muḥtāj* (Beirut: Al-Maktabah al-Islāmiyyah, 1994), 68; Ibn Hajar al-'Asqalānī, *Al-Talkhīṣ al-ḥabīr*, 2098; al-Suyūṭī, *Jam' al-jawāmi'*, 3345/27; al-'Irāqī, *Takhrīj aḥādīth Iḥyā' 'ulūm al-dīn*, 3672. The various transmissions have problems.

There is a sound hadith likening the Companions ﷺ to stars: "The stars are a source of security for the sky [...] and my Companions are a source of security for the Umma..." Muslim, 2531 #207; al-Suyūṭī, *Al-Jāmi' al-ṣaghīr*, 11748; *Jam' al-jawāmi'*, 3345/27, 12042/45.

204 Ismā'īl bin Muḥammad al-'Ajlūnī, *Kashf al-khafā'* (Cairo: Maktabat al-Qudsī, 1351), 489.

سِـتَّةِ أَشْـهُرٍ. هَذَا إِذَا لَمْ يَنْوِ شَـيْئًا مُعَيَّنًا مِنَ الزَّمَانِ. فَإِنْ نَوَاهُ حُمِلَ عَلَيْهِ بِاتِّفَاقِ الأَئِمَةِ الأَرْبَعَةِ.

Al-Shāfi'ī's approach [*madhhab*] is to interpret the duration [*al-ḥīn*] as the passing of an instant of time. Mālik's approach is the same as 'Uthmān's opinion. Abū Ḥanīfah's and Aḥmad's approach is to interpret the duration as six months. This is provided that the individual did not intend some specific duration of time; and in that case, it would be interpreted according to it [i.e. whatever he intended]—which the four Imams agreed upon.

PROTECTING THE UNIVERSALS [وُجوبُ حِفظِ الكُلّيّاتِ الخمسِ]

وَمِمَّـا يَجِـبُ وُجُـوْبَ عَمَلٍ حِفْـظُ الكُلِّيَّـاتِ، وَهِيَ: الدِّيْـنُ، وَالنَّفْسُ، وَالنَّسَـبُ، وَالمَالُ، وَالعِرْضُ، وَالعَقْلُ.

It is also obligatory to act towards protecting the universals [*al-kulliyyāt*] and they are: religion, persons, lineage, property, honour, and the intellect.[205]

فَالدِّيْنُ هُوَ مَا شَرَعَهُ اللّٰهُ لِعِبَادِهِ مِنَ الأَحْكَامِ. وَحِفْظُهُ يَكُوْنُ بِصِيَانَتِهِ عَنْ ارتِـكَابِ المُكَفِّرَاتِ، وَعَنْ انْتِهَاكِ حُرْمَـةِ الحُرُمَاتِ بِأَنْ يَفْعَلَهَا غَيْرَ مُبَالٍ بِحُرْمَتِهَا، وَعَنْ انْتِهَاكِ وُجُوْبِ الواجِبَاتِ بِأَنْ يَتْرُكَهَا غَيْرَ مُبَالٍ بِوُجُوْبِهَا.

The religion [*al-dīn*] refers to the rulings that Allah has legislated for His servants. Its protection consists of preserving oneself from committing anything that causes disbelief, and from violating the unlawfulness of unlawful acts by performing them without concern for their being unlawful; and from violating the obligatoriness of

205 *Jawharah*, 127; *Tuḥfah*, 766.

obligatory acts by leaving them undone without concern for their being obligatory.[206]

وَحِفْظُ النَّفْسِ العَاقِلَةِ يَكُوْنُ بِصِيَانَتِهَا عَمَّا يَضُرُّهَا. وَلِحِفْظِهَا شُرِّعَ القِصَاصُ فِي النَّفْسِ وَالطَّرَفِ وَنَحْوِهِمَا.

Protecting the rational person [*al-nafs al-'āqilah*] consists of preserving it from everything that harms it. The reciprocal punishments for killing and injuring and the like were legislated for its protection.[207]

وَحِفْظُ المَالِ يَكُوْنُ بِعَدَمِ التَّعَدِّي بِفِعْلٍ غَيْرِ المَأْذُوْنِ فِيْهِ، وَالمُرَادُ بِهِ كُلُّ مَا يَحِلُّ(208) تَمَلُّكُهُ شَرْعًا وَإِنْ قَلَّ. وَلِحِفْظِهِ شُرِّعَ حَدُّ السَّرِقَةِ وَحَدُّ قَطْعِ الطَّرِيْقِ وَضَمَانُ المُتْلَفَاتِ. وَمِثْلُ المَالِ الإِخْتِصَاصُ فِي حُرْمَةِ التَّعَدِّي فِيْهِ لَا فِي الحَدِّ وَالضَّمَانِ.

Protecting property [*al-māl*] consists of not maliciously performing an act that one does not have permission to perform. It [i.e. property, *māl*] means everything that, according to the Sacred Law, is conceivable to own—even if it is a small amount. The prescribed punishments for theft and highway robbery, and compensation for losses, were legislated for its protection. Personal possessions [*ikhtiṣāṣāt*] are similar to property, it being unlawful to transgress against them, though not with respect to the prescribed punishment and compensation for losses.[209]

ثُمَّ النَّسَبُ هُوَ الإِرْتِبَاطُ الَّذِي يَكُوْنُ بَيْنَ الوَالِدِ وَالوَلَدِ. وَلِحِفْظِهِ شُرِّعَ حَدُّ الزِّنَا.

---

206 *Jawharah*, 127; *Tuḥfah*, 769.

207 *Jawharah*, 127; *Tuḥfah*, 766, 770.

208 Ustaz Zainul Abidin mentioned that A has «يحمل», and perhaps what is mentioned here is better.

209 *Jawharah*, 127; *Tuḥfah*, 771.

Lineage [*al-nasab*] is the connection between the parent and the child. The prescribed punishment for fornication was legislated for its protection.[210]

وَالعِرْضُ وَهُوَ مَحَلُّ المَدْحِ وَالذَّمِ مِنْ الإِنْسَانِ، تَتَقَوَّى بِهِ الأَفْعَالُ الحَمِيْدَةُ وَتَزْدَرِي بِهِ الأَفْعَالُ القَبِيْحَةُ. وَلِحِفْظِهِ شُرِّعَ الحَدُّ عَلَى مَنْ قَذَفَ العَفِيْفَ وَالتَّعْزِيْرُ عَلَى مَنْ قَذَفَ غَيْرَهُ.

Honour [*al-ʿirḍ*] (the trait an individual possesses that is associated with praise and blame) is strengthened through praiseworthy acts and disgraced through ugly acts. The prescribed punishment for accusing chaste individuals of fornication, and the disciplinary punishment for accusing others, are legislated for its protection.[211]

والعَقْـلُ نُوْرٌ رُوْحَانِيٌّ، بِهِ تُدْرِكُ النَّفْـسُ العُلُوْمَ الضَّرُوْرِيَّةَ النَّظَرِيَّةَ. وَلِحِفْظِهِ شُرِّعَ حَدُّ الشُّرْبِ وَالدِّيةُ عَلَى مَنْ أَذْهَبَهُ بِجِنَايَةٍ.

The intellect [*al-ʿaql*] is a spiritual light through which the [rational] person perceives necessary and speculative knowledge.[212] The prescribed punishment for drinking intoxicants, and blood-money being owed from whomever causes its loss, are legislated for its protection.[213]

وَأَوْكَدُ هَذِهِ الأُمُوْرِ حِفْظُ الدِّيْنِ، ثُمَّ حِفْظُ النَّفْسِ، ثُمَّ حِفْظُ النَّسَبِ، ثُمَّ حِفْظُ العَقْلِ، ثُمَّ المَالِ فِي مَرْتَبَةِ العِرْضِ.

The most emphatic of these matters is protecting the religion, then the self, then lineage, then the intellect, then property (in the same rank as reputation).[214]

210 *Jawharah*, 127; *Tuḥfah*, 772.
211 *Jawharah*, 127; *Tuḥfah*, 774.
212 *Jawharah*, 95; *Tuḥfah*, 603.
213 *Jawharah*, 127; *Tuḥfah*, 773.
214 *Jawharah*, 127; *Tuḥfah*, 767.

ACTIONS OBLIGATORY TO ABANDON

[وُجوبُ تَخليَّةِ النَّفسِ عَن الصِّفاتِ المَذمومَةِ]

BOASTING

[تَرْكُ التَّسميعِ]

وَمِمَّا يَجِبُ وُجُوبَ عَمَلٍ تَرْكُ التَّسْمِيْعِ، وَهُوَ أَنْ يَعْمَلَ العَمَلَ وَحْدَهُ، ثُمَّ يُخْبِرَ بَهِ النَّاسَ لِأَجْلِ تَعْظِيْمِهِمْ لَهُ أَوْ لِأَجْلِ جَلْبِ خَيْرٍ مِنْهُمْ.

Among what is necessary to obligatorily act upon is abandoning speaking of one's deeds [*al-tasmīʿ*]. It is performing an action while alone and then telling people about it so they venerate him for it or to attract some goodness from them.[215]

قَالَ سَيِّدِي عَلِيٌّ الخَوَّاصُ لِأَصْحَابِهِ: «احْذُرُوْا مِنَ التَّسْمِيْعِ بِأَعْمَالِكُمْ؛ فَإِنَّهُ يُبْطِلُهَا كَالرِّيَاءِ عَلَى حَدٍّ سَوَاءٍ، لَكِنَّ لِلتَّسْمِيْعِ دَوَاءٌ، وَهُوَ أَنْ يَنْدَمَ العَبْدُ عَلَى ذَلِكَ وَيَتُوْبَ مِنْ ذَلِكَ تَوْبَةً صَادِقَةً بِأَنَّهُ لَا يَعُوْدُ يُسَمِّعُ أَحَدًا مِنَ النَّاسِ بِعَمَلٍ مِنْ أَعْمَالِهِ؛ إِذْ التَّوْبَةُ الصَّادِقَةُ تَمْحُوْ تِلْكَ الزَّلَّةَ. فَإِذَا تَابَ كَذَلِكَ رَجَعَ العَمَلُ صَحِيْحًا بِمَشِيْئَةِ اللهِ تَعَالَى. وَمَثَلُ ذَلِكَ كَمَثَلِ رَجُلٍ كَانَ صَحِيْحَ الجِسْمِ ثُمَّ طَرَأَ عَلَيْهِ مَرَضٌ أَفْسَدَ صِحَّتَهُ، فَاسْتَعْمَلَ دَوَاءً نَافِعًا، فَأَزَالَ اللَّهُ تَعَالَى بِهِ ذَلِكَ المَرَضَ وَعَادَ الجِسْمُ بِفَضْلِ اللَّهِ تَعَالَى إِلَى حَالَ صِحَّتِهِ». فَعُلِمَ أَنَّ لِلتَّسْمِيْعِ دَوَاءٌ بِخِلَافِ الرِّيَاءِ؛ لِأَنَّهُ يُفْسِدُ العَمَلَ مِنْ أَصْلِهِ.

كَذَا قَالَ الشَّعْرَانِيُّ.

[Imam al-Shaʿrānī wrote in *Al-Minaḥ al-saniyyah*]

---

215 *Jawharat*, 140; *Tuḥfat*, 868.

My Master ʿAlī al-Khawwāṣ said to his companions:

'Take caution against boasting of your deeds since it voids them just like showing off [riyā]. They [i.e. boasting and showing off] are equal, except that there is a treatment for boasting, which is that the servant truthfully regret doing what he did and repent from it by not resuming to boast to anyone about any of his deeds, since true repentance erases that slip, so if he repents then that act returns to being sound by the will of Allah (Most High is He). The likeness of that [i.e. repentance] is as the likeness of a man with a healthy body who suddenly becomes sick and it spoils his health, so he uses beneficial medicine—thus Allah (Most High is He) removes that sickness and the body returns, through the generosity of Allah (Most High is He), to its healthy state.'

"Consequently, it is known that there is a treatment for boasting. [This is] in contrast to showing off, since it [showing off] destroys actions from their start."[216]

This is what al-Shaʿrānī said.

SHOWING OFF [تَرْكُ الرِّيَاءِ]

وَهُوَ [أَي: الرِّيَاءُ(217)] قِسْمَانِ: جَلِيٌّ وَخَفِيٌّ.

[Showing off, *riyā*] is of two divisions: outward and hidden.

فَالأَوَّلُ أَنْ يَعْمَلَ الطَّاعَةَ بِحَضْرَةِ النَّاسِ لَا غَيْرُ، فَإِنْ خَلَا بِنَفْسِهِ لَا يَفْعَلُ شَيْئًا.

216 Al-Shaʿrānī, *Al-Minaḥ al-saniyyah*.
217 This is understood from the context.

The first [obvious showing off] is that one performs acts of obedience only when people are present and, when alone, he does nothing at all.

وَالثَّانِي أَنْ يَفْعَلَهَا مُطْلَقًا -حَضَرَ النَّاسُ أَوْ لَا- لَكِنْ يَفْرَحُ عِنْدَ حُضُورِهِمْ.

The second [hidden showing off] is performing it without restriction (whether people are present or not), though being happy when they are present.[218]

قَالَ سَيِّدِي عَبْدُ الوَهَّابِ الشَّعْرَانِيُّ: «وَمِنْ دَقَائِقِ الرِّيَاءِ اِسْتِحْلَاءُ العِبَادَةِ لِأَنَّ النَّفْسَ لَا تَسْتَلِذُّ بِعِبَادَةٍ إِلَّا أَنْ وَافَقَتْ هَوَاهَا. وَلَوْ أَنَّهَا خَلَصَتْ عَنِ الهَوَى لَثَقُلَتْ عَلَيْهَا».

My master 'Abd al-Wahhāb al-Sha'rānī said that[219] "one of the subtle [forms] of showing off is being delighted by worship, since the *nafs* takes no pleasure in worship unless it matches its whims. And when it [worship] is free of its [whims], it becomes burdensome to it [the *nafs*]."

وَمِنْهَا: العَمَلُ لِلَّهِ وَلِشَيْءٍ آخَرَ. وَقَدْ أَجْمَعَ العَارِفُوْنَ عَلَى أَنَّ تَوْحِيْدَ القَصْدِ وَاجِبٌ لِيَجْعَلُوْا لَهُمْ هَمًّا وَاحِدًا مُتَعَلِّقًا بِوَاحِدٍ لَا يُشَمُّ مِنْ تَوْحِيْدِ اللَّهِ تَعَالَى رَائِحَةٌ.

[Showing off] includes performing an act for Allah and for something else. The gnostics [*al-'ārifūn*] reached a consensus that having a unified intent is obligatory, so they would have a single concern linked to one thing so [their] monotheism of Allah (Most High is He) is odourless.

218 The two types: *Jawharah*, 140; *Tuḥfah*, 871.

219 Most of the examples mentioned in this section come from 'Abd al-Wahhāb al-Sha'rānī's *Al-Minaḥ al-saniyyah*.

وَمِنْهَا: اِدِّعَاءُ المَقَامَاتِ قَبْلِ بُلُوْغِهَا أَوْ بَعْدَ بُلُوْغِهَا وَلَمْ يُؤْذَنْ لَهُمْ فِي إِظْهَارِهَا.

[Showing off] includes claiming to have attained [spiritual] stations before arriving at them, or after arriving at them but without having been given permission to display them.

وَمِنْهَا: مَحَبَّةُ اِطِّلَاعِ النَّاسِ عَلَى العِبَادَةِ وَغَيْرِهَا.

[Showing off] includes loving that people observe one's [acts of] worship and other deeds.

وَمِنْهَا: تَرْكُ العَمَلِ مِنْ أَجْلِ النَّاسِ؛ فَمَنْ عَزَمَ عَلَى عِبَادَةٍ وَتَرَكَهَا مَخَافَةَ أَنْ يَرَاهُ النَّاسُ فَهُوَ مُرَاءٍ لِأَنَّهُ تَرَكَهَا مِنْ أَجْلِ النَّاسِ. أَمَّا لَوْ تَرَكَهَا لِيَفْعَلَهَا فِي الخَلْوَةِ فَهَذَا مُسْتَحَبٌّ إِلَّا أَنْ تَكُوْنَ فَرِيْضَةً أَوْ زَكَاةً وَاجِبَةً أَوْ يَكُوْنَ مِمَّنَ يُقْتَدَى بِهِ؛ فَالجَهْرُ فِي ذَلِكَ أَفْضَلُ.

[Showing off] includes abandoning actions for people. Thus, whoever resolves to perform an act of worship and abandons it out of fear that people will see it has shown off since he abandoned it for people. However, if he abandoned it in order to perform it in seclusion, this is recommended unless it is an obligatory act [of prayer], obligatory zakat, or he is someone who is followed [by others as an example]—in which case it is best [for him] to perform it publicly.

وَمِنْهَا: حِكَايَةُ الأَعْمَالِ الصَّالِحَةِ الَّتِي وَقَعَتْ فِي أَزْمَانٍ مَضَتْ وَلَمْ يَشْعُرْ بِهَا أَحَدٌ إِلَّا لِغَرَضٍ شَرْعِيٍّ، فَإِنَّ حِكَايَتَهَا بِغَيْرِ غَرَضٍ شَرْعِيٍّ يَرُدُّهَا إِلَى صُوْرَةِ الرِّيَاءِ بِهَا حَالَ عَمَلِهَا.

[Showing off] includes speaking of pious acts that happened in the past that no one was aware of (unless [one mentions them] for a religious purpose), since speaking about them without a religious purpose turns them into a form of showing off at the time they were performed.

وَمِنْهَا: قَطْعُ المِزَاحِ المُبَاحِ إِذَا دَخَلَ مَنْ يُسْتَحَى مِنْهُ بِغَيْرِ نِيَّةٍ صَالِحَةٍ. فَإِنَّ خَرْقَ نَامُوْسِ العَبْدِ عِنْدَ مَنْ يُسْتَحَى مِنْهُ أَوْلَى مِنْ اِرْتِكَابِ صِفَةِ النِّفَاقِ.

[Showing off] includes interrupting permissible jesting when a person whose presence calls for reserved behaviour enters without having a sound intention [for its interruption], since violating the normal behaviour that a servant should have with a person whose presence calls for revered behaviour is better than assuming the quality of hypocrisy.

وَمِنْهَا: الزِّيَادَةُ فِي الإِطْرَاقِ وَالخُشُوْعِ لِدُخُوْلِ أَحَدٍ مِنَ الأَكَابِرِ وَغَيْرِهِمْ.

[Showing off] includes excessively lowering one's head or acting more humble than necessary when a senior or someone else enters.

PRIDE [تَرْكُ العُجْبِ]

وَمِمَّا يَجِبُ وُجُوْبَ عَمَلٍ: تَرْكُ العُجْبِ، وَهُوَ رُؤْيَةُ العِبَادَةِ وَاسْتِعْظَامُهَا كَمَا يُعْجَبُ العَابِدُ بِعِبَادَتِهِ وَالعَالِمُ بِعِلْمِهِ، فَهٰذَا حَرَامٌ غَيْرُ مُفْسِدٍ لِلطَّاعَةِ، وَكَذٰلِكَ الرِّيَاءُ. وَإِنَّمَا هُوَ مُحْبِطٌ لِلثَّوَابِ فَقَطْ مَعَ وُقُوْعِ العَمَلِ صَحِيحًا.

Abandoning pride [*al-'ujb*] is among what is necessary to obligatorily act upon. It is seeing acts of worship and thinking highly of them, such as a devotee taking pride in his worship and a scholar [taking pride] in his knowledge.[220] This is unlawful without voiding acts of obedience, as is showing off.[221] Indeed: it just reduces rewards, while the act remains valid.

وَإِنَّمَا حَرُمَ العُجْبُ لِأَنَّهُ سُوْءُ أَدَبٍ مَعَ اللَّهِ تَعَالَى؛ إِذْ لَا يَنْبَغِي لِلعَبْدِ أَنْ يَسْتَعْظِمَ مَا يَتَقَرَّبُ بِهِ لِسَيِّدِهِ، بَلْ يَسْتَصْغِرُهُ بِالنِّسْبَةِ لِعَظَمَةِ سَيِّدِهِ.

Pride is unlawful out of it having bad etiquette with Allah (Most High is He) since the slave should not think highly of what he does to draw close to his master. Rather, he should think little of it relative to the greatness of his master.[222]

ARROGANCE [تَرْكُ الكِبرِ]

وَمِنْ ذَلِكَ: تَرْكُ الكِبْرِ، وَهُوَ بَطَرِ الحَقِّ، وَغَمْصِ الخَلْقِ. فَمَعْنَى «بَطَرِ الحَقِّ»: رَدُّ الحَقِّ عَلَى قَائِلِهِ، أَي: عَدَمُ قَبُوْلِ الحَقِّ مِنْهُ، وَمَعْنَى «وَغَمْصُ الخَلْقِ»، أَي: اِحْتِقَارُهُمْ وَالتَّهَاوُنُ بِهِمْ.

Abandoning arrogance [*al-kibr*] is among [what is necessary to obligatorily act upon]. It is disregarding the truth [*baṭar al-ḥaqq*] and having contempt for people.[223] "Disregarding the truth" means throwing the truth back on the person who says it (i.e. not accepting the truth from him).[224] "Having contempt for people" means looking down on them [disdaining them] and scorning them.

---

220 *Jawharah*, 135; *Tuḥfah*, 814.
221 *Jawharah*, 140; *Tuḥfah*, 868.
222 *Jawharah*, 135; *Tuḥfah*, 814.
223 *Jawharah*, 135; *Tuḥfah*, 816.
224 *Jawharah*, 135; *Tuḥfah*, 818.

فَالتَّجَمُّلُ بِالمَلَابِسِ وَنَحْوِهَا لَيْسَ كِبْرًا[225]، بَلْ يَكُوْنُ مَنْدُوْبًا فِي الصَّلَوَاتِ وَالجَمَاعَاتِ وَنَحْوِهَا، وَفِي حَقِّ المَرْأَةِ لِزَوْجِهَا، وَفِي حَقِّ العُلَمَاءِ لِتَعْظِيْمِ العِلْمِ فِي نُفُوْسِ النَّاسِ.

Wearing beautiful clothing and the like is not arrogance. Indeed, doing so is recommended for prayers, Fridays and the like; for women for the sake of their husbands; and for scholars to magnify [the status of] knowledge in the hearts of people.[226]

وَيَكُوْنُ وَاجِبًا فِي حَقِّ وُلَاةِ الأُمُوْرِ وَغَيْرِهِمْ إِذَا تَوَقَّفَ عَلَيْهِ تَنْفِيْذُ الوَاجِبِ. فَإِنَّ الهَيْئَةَ المُزْرِيَةَ لَا تَصْلُحُ مَعَهَا مَصَالِحُ العَامَّةِ فِي العُصُوْرِ[227] المُتَأَخِّرِ لِمَا طُبِعَتْ عَلَيْهِ النُّفُوْسُ الآنَ مِنَ التَّعْظِيْمِ بِالصُّوَرِ، عَكْسُ مَا كَانَ عَلَيْهِ السَّلَفُ الصَّالِحُ مِنْ التَّعْظِيْمِ بِالدِّيْنِ وَالتَّقْوَى.

[Wearing beautiful clothing] is obligatory for those with public responsibilities and others when it is a dependency for executing a duty. This is because having a contemptible appearance is not conducive for the general welfare in the late epoch since people's egos are disposed to venerate based on appearances—which is opposite to the way of the pious predecessors of venerating based on religiosity and keeping one's duty to Allah.[228]

وَيَكُوْنُ حَرَامًا إِذَا كَانَ وَسِيْلَةً لِمُحَرَّمٍ، وَمَكْرُوْهًا إِذَا كَانَ وَسِيْلَةً لِمَكْرُوْهٍ، وَمُبَاحًا إِذَا خَلَا عَنْ هَذِهِ الأَسْبَابِ.

[Wearing beautiful clothing] is unlawful when it is a means to what

225 Ustaz Zainul Abidin mentioned that A has «كبر», and perhaps what is mentioned here is better since it matches the rules of Arabic grammar.

226 *Jawharah*, 135; *Tuḥfah*, 817.

227 Ustaz Zainul Abidin mentioned that A has «العصر», and perhaps what is mentioned here is better.

228 *Jawharah*, 135; *Tuḥfah*, 817.

is unlawful, offensive when it is a means to what is offensive, and permissible when it is free from these causes.[229]

ENVY

[تَرْكُ الحَسَدِ]

وَمِنْ ذَلِكَ: تَرْكُ الحَسَدِ، وَهُوَ تَمَنِّي زَوَالِ نِعْمَةِ الغَيْرِ، سَوَاءٌ تَمَنَّاهَا لِنَفْسِهِ أَوْ لَا؛ بِأَنْ تَمَنَّى اِنْتِقَالَهَا عَنْ غَيْرِهِ(230) لِغَيْرِهِ. وَهَذَا أَخَسُّ الأَخِسَّاءِ؛ لِأَنَّهُ بَاعَ آخِرَتَهُ بِدُنْيَا غَيْرِهِ، بِخِلَافِ مَا إِذَا تَمَنَّى مِثْلَ نِعْمَةِ الغَيْرِ؛ فَإِنَّهُ غِبْطَةٌ مَحْمُودَةٌ فِي الخَيْرِ.

Abandoning envy [*al-ḥasad*] is among [what is necessary to obligatorily act upon]. It is wanting someone else's blessing to end—whether one wishes it for oneself or not [such as] by wanting it to be transferred from someone else to another person. This is the most despicable of things since he [has] sold his afterlife for someone else's worldly life. [This] is in contrast to if he had wished for a blessing like what someone has, for it is appreciation of another's fortune [*al-ghibṭah*] and it is praiseworthy for good things.[231]

TALE-BEARING

[تَرْكُ النَّمِيمَةِ]

وَمِنْهُ: تَرْكُ النَّمِيمَةِ. قَالَ الغَزَالِيُّ: وَحَدُّهَا كَشْفُهُ مَا يُكْرَهُ كَشْفُهُ سَوَاءٌ كَانَ الكَشْفُ بِالقَوْلِ أَوِ الكِتَابَةِ أَوِ الرَّمْزِ أَوْ نَحْوِهَا، وَسَوَاءٌ كَانَ المَنْقُولُ مِنَ الأَقْوَالِ أَوْ مِنَ الأَعْمَالِ أَوْ مِنَ الأَحْوَالِ، وَسَوَاءٌ كَانَ عَيْبًا أَوْ غَيْرَهُ.

229 *Jawharah*, 135; *Tuḥfah*, 817.

230 Ustaz Zainul Abidin mentioned that A has «غيرها», and perhaps what is mentioned here is better.

231 *Jawharah*, 135; *Tuḥfah*, 821.

وَقَالَ النَّوَوِيُّ: «حَقِيْقَةُ النَّمِيْمَةِ إِفْشَاءُ السِّرِ وَهَتْكُ السِّتْرِ عَمَّا يُكْرَهُ كَشْفُهُ».

Abandoning tale-bearing [*al-namīmah*] is among [what is necessary to obligatorily act upon].[232] Al-Ghazālī said that its definition is to expose what one despises to be exposed, whether it is exposed via speech, writing, gesture, or the like; and whether what is communicated is words, actions, or states; and whether it was a defect or something else.[233]

Al-Nawawī said that the true reality of tale-bearing is spreading secrets and revealing what one despises to be exposed.[234]

BACKBITING [تركُ الغِيْبَةِ]

ومنهُ: اِجْتِنَابُ الغِيْبَةِ، وَهِيَ كُلُّ مَا أَفْهَمْتَ بِهِ غَيْرَكَ نُقْصَانَ مُسْلِمٍ بِلَفْظِكَ أَوْ كِتَابِكَ وَأَشَرْتَ إِلَيْهِ بِعَيْنِكَ أَوْ يَدِكَ أَوْ رَأْسِكَ أَوْ نحوِ ذَلِكَ، سَوَاءٌ كَانَ ذَلِكَ فِي بَدَنِهِ أَوْ دِيْنِهِ أَوْ دُنْيَاهُ أَوْ وَلَدِهِ أَوْ وَالِدِهِ أَوْ زَوْجَتِهِ أَوْ خَادِمِهِ أَوْ حِرْفَتِهِ أَوْ لَوْنِهِ أَوْ مَرْكُوْبِهِ أَوْ عِمَامَتِهِ أَوْ ثَوْبِهِ أَوْ غَيْرِ ذَلِكَ مِمَّا يَتَعَلَّقُ بِهِ.

Avoiding backbiting [*al-ghībah*] is among [what is necessary to obligatorily act upon]. It is anything that someone else can understand

232 *Jawharah*, 134; *Tuḥfah*, 801.

233 Quoted in *Jawharah*, 134; *Tuḥfah*, 801. The original source for the passage is al-Ghazālī, *Iḥyā' 'ulūm al-dīn* (Dār al-Ma'rifah, n.d.), 3:156. However, the wording given here matches what is in Imām al-Nawawī's *Al-Adhkār* (Dār Ibn Ḥazm, 2004/1425), p552 #1789.

234 al-Nawawī, *Al-Adhkār*, p348; *Al-Minhāj sharḥ Ṣaḥīḥ Muslim bin al-Hajjāj* (Beirut: Dār Iḥyā' al-Turāth al-'Arabī, 1392), 2:113.

from you to indicate a deficiency in another Muslim, whether it be your utterances, your writing, your pointing to them with your eyes or hand or head, or the like; and whether this [defect] is related to his body, his religion, his worldly life, his parent, his child, his wife, his servant, his profession, his colour, his conveyance, his turban, his clothes, or other things that are linked with him.[235]

وتَحْـرُمُ الغِيْبَـةِ فِـي الخَلْـوَةِ دُوْنَ حُضُوْرِ أَحَدٍ. وَكَذَا بِالقَلْـبِ فَقَطْ. فَإنَّهَا بِالقَلْبِ مُحَرَّمَةٌ كَهِيَ بِاللِّسَانِ. وَمَحَلُّ ذَلِكَ فِي غَيْرِ مَنْ شَاهَدَ، وَأَمَّا مَنْ شَاهَدَ فَيُعْذَرُ فِي الاِعْتِقَادِ حَيْنَئِذٍ. نَعَمْ، يَنْبَغِي أَنْ يَحْمِلَهُ عَلَى أَنَّهُ تَابَ.

Backbiting is unlawful when alone without anyone being present, just as it is when it is only in the heart, for backbiting in the heart is forbidden just as it is via the tongue. The context for this is for someone who did not witness [the act directly]. As for someone who did witness [it], his beliefs are excusable in that case. Though he [the witness] should assume that the person has repented.[236]

وَالغِيْبَـةُ مُحَرَّمَـةُ بِالإِجْمَاعِ، وَإِنَّمَا اِخْتُلِفَ فِـي مَرْتَبَتِهَا. وَالمُعتَمَدُ مَا جَزَمَ بِـهِ ابْـنُ حَجَـرِ الهَيْتَمِيُّ، مِنْ أَنَّ غِيْبَـةَ العَالِمِ وَحَامِلِ القُـرْآنِ كَبِيْرَةٌ وَغِيْبَةَ غَيْرِهِمَا صَغِيْرَةٌ.

Backbiting is unlawful according to consensus.[237] What they disagreed about was its rank.[238] The relied upon opinion is what Ibn Ḥajar al-Haytamī was convinced of: That backbiting scholars and bearers of the Quran is a major sin [*kabīrah*], and [backbiting] others is a lesser sin [*ṣaghīrah*].[239]

---

235 *Jawharah*, 134; *Tuḥfah*, 804.
236 *Jawharah*, 134; *Tuḥfah*, 804.
237 *Jawharah*, 134; *Tuḥfah*, 804.
238 *Jawharah*, 134; *Tuḥfah*, 806.
239 *Jawharah*, 134; *Tuḥfah*, 806.

وَكَمَا يَحْرُمُ عَلَى المُغْتَابِ ذِكْرُ الغِيْبَةِ، يَحْرُمُ عَلَى السَّامِعِ إِسْمَاعُهَا وَإِقْرَارُهَا. فَيَجِبُ عَلَى كُلِّ مَنْ سَمِعَ إِنْسَانًا يَذْكُرُ غِيْبَةً مُحَرَّمَةً أَنْ يَنْهَاهُ إِنْ لَمْ يَخَفْ ضَرَرًا ظَاهِرًا.

Just as it is unlawful for the backbiter to mention the backbiting, it is also unlawful for the one who hears it to listen to it and affirm it. Thus, it is obligatory for everyone who hears a person mentioning unlawful backbiting to forbid him from doing so if he does not fear manifest harm.[240]

وَقَدْ وَرَدَ فِي الحَدِيْثِ: «مَنْ رَدَّ غِيْبَةَ مُسْلِمٍ رَدَّ اللَّهُ النَّارَ عَنْ وَجْهِهِ يَوْمَ القِيَامَةِ»، فَإِنْ لَمْ يَسْتَطِعْ إِزَالَتَهَا بِاليَدِ وَلَا بِاللِّسَانِ فَارَقَ ذَلِكَ المَجْلِسَ وَلَا يُخَلِّصُ الإِنْكَارُ بِحَسَبِ الظَّاهِرِ؛ فَإِنْ قَالَ لِسَانُهُ: «أُسْكُتْ» وَهُوَ يَشْتَهِي بِقَلْبِهِ إِسْتِمْرَارَهُ فَذَلِكَ نِفَاقٌ، فَلَا بُدَّ مِنْ كَرَاهَتِهَا بِقَلْبِهِ.

It was transmitted in the hadith that "Whoever repels the backbiting of a Muslim, Allah will repel the fire from his face on Judgment Day."[241] Thus, if one is unable to stop it [the backbiting] with their hand or tongue, he departs from the assembly.[242]

Appearances alone are not enough when rebuking. If one says, "Be quiet!" with his tongue while, in his heart, he desires its continuance, this is hypocrisy and one must dislike it in his heart.[243]

---

240 *Jawharah*, 134; *Tuḥfah*, 806.

241 I could not locate this specific phrasing. The closest match I could locate is "Whoever protects his brother's honour...". Aḥmad, 27583; al-Tirmidhī, 1931; al-Bayhaqī, *Shu'ab al-īmān*, 7229;

242 *Jawharah*, 134; *Tuḥfah*, 807.

243 This passage is from Imām al-Nawawī's *Al-Adhkār*, 1:540 (1728); there, he attributes "this is hypocrisy..." to Imām al-Ghazālī's *Iḥyā'*, 3:146.

CLOSING REMARKS

[الخَاتِمَةُ]

(٣٥) سَـمَّـيْـتُـهَـا نُـقَـاوَةَ الـعَـقِـيْـدَةْ ٭ أَبْيَاتُهَا لَوْ يَنْبَغِي أَنْ تُقْصَدَهْ

(35) I named it "The Select Creed," * Its verses ought to be sought

أَي: سَمَّيتُ هَذِهِ المَنْظُوْمَةَ «نُقَاوَةَ العَقِيْدَةِ»، أَي: خِيَارَهَا؛ فَذَلِكَ يَنْبَغِي أَنْ تُقْصَدَ. وَأَبْيَاتُهَا سِتَّةٌ وَثَلَاثُوْنَ بَيْتًا.

Meaning: I named this versification "*Nuqāwat al-ʿaqīdah*," i.e. the best of it, so it ought to be sought out. Its verses [number] thirty-six verses.

قَوْلُهُ: «أَنْ تُقْصَدَ»، مَبْنِيٌّ لِلمَجْهُوْلِ، وَالهَاءُ لِلوَقْفِ.

Him [the versifier] saying, "ought to be sought [*an tuqṣadah*]" is in the passive tense, and the "*hā*'" is for stopping [at the end of the stanza instead of the full pronoun "*hā*'"].

(٣٦) تَارِيْخُهَا غَرْقٌ فَيَا رَبِّ الْطُفِ ٭ بِـنَـا وَوَالِـدٍ عَـقِـبٍ وَاسْـعَـفِ

(36) Its history is "*gharq*," so, O Lord, be gentle * To us, and parents, progeny, and give aid

أَي: وَقْتُ نَظْمِ هَذِهِ المَنْظُوْمَةِ فِي عَامٍ أَلْفٍ وَثَلَاثِمائَةٍ.

Meaning: the time of versifying this versification is the year 1300 [i.e. the values for the letters *ghayn, rā',* and *qāf* are (respectively) 1000, 200, and 100, totalling 1300, so 1300 AH].

وَمَعْنَـى: «اُلْطُـفْ»، أَي: وَفِّقْ عَلَى أَدَاءِ الطَّاعَاتِ، وَاعْصِمْ مِنَ الذُّنُوْبِ وَالبَلَايَا، وَارْزُقْ.

The meaning of [the phrase] "be gentle [*ulṭuf*]" is "Grant success in carrying out obedience, protect from sins and trials, and be kind."

وَمَعْنَي: «وَاسْعَفْ»، أَي: اِقْضِ حَاجَتِي، وَأَعِنِّي عَلَى جَمِيْعِ الأُمُوْرِ.

[The phrase] "give aid [*wa-s'af*]" means "fulfil my needs and take care of all matters."

وَمَعْنَي: «عَقِبَ الوَالِدِ»، وَلَدُ الوَلَدِ.

[The phrase] "a parent's progeny [*'aqib al-wālid*]" is the child's child [i.e. the parent's grandchildren].

(٣٧) وَالحَمْدُ لِلَّهْ صَلِّ سَلِّمْ لِلنَّبِيْ * وَالآلِ وَالصَّحْبِ أُوْلِي المَنَاقِبِ

(37) Praise to Allah, pray and bless the Prophet * And the folk and Companions with the most virtues.

أَي: المَفَاخِرُ، وَهِيَ الصِّفَاتُ المَحْمُوْدَةُ.

["Virtues",] i.e. glorious qualities, which are praiseworthy traits.

وَإِنَّمَا أَتَى النَّاظِمُ بِالحَمْدَلَةِ أَدَاءً لِلشُّكْرِ الوَاجِبِ عَلَيْهِ حَيْثُ وُفِّقَ لِلتَّمَامِ. وَإِنَّمَا أَتَى بِالصَّلَاةِ وَالسَّلَامِ فِي أَوَّلِ كِتَابِهِ وَفِي آخِرِهِ رَجَاءً لِقَبُوْلِ مَا بَيْنَهُمَا؛ لِأَنَّ الصَّلَاةَ عَلَى النَّبِيِّ ﷺ مَقْبُوْلَةٌ لَا مَرْدُوْدَةٌ، وَاللَّهُ أَكْرَمُ مِنْ أَنْ يَقْبَلَ الصَّلَاتَيْنِ وَيَرُدَّ مَا بَيْنَهُمَا.

The versifier brought the *ḥamdalah* to express the gratitude that is obligatory for him for being granted success to complete [the verses]. He mentioned prayers and blessings at the beginning and the end of his writing out of hope that what comes between them will be accepted, since prayers upon the Prophet ﷺ are accepted and never rejected—and Allah is more generous than to accept the two prayers but reject what came between them.

وَصَلَّى اللَّهُ وَسَلَّمَ وَشَرَّفَ وَكَرَّمَ عَلَى النَّبِيِّ سَيِّدِ الأَوَّلِيْنَ وَالآخِرِيْنَ، وَعَلَى آلِهِ وَصَحْبِهِ أَجْمَعِيْنَ كُلَّمَا ذَكَرَهُ الذَّاكِرُوْنَ وَغَفَلَ عَنْ ذِكْرِهِ الغَافِلُوْنَ، وَسَلَامٌ عَلَى المُرْسَلِيْنَ، وَالحَمْدُ لِلَّهِ رَبِّ العَالَمِيْنَ.

May Allah pray upon, bless, honour, and venerate the Prophet, the master of the first and the last, and his folk and Companions, all together. [May these happen] every time the mindful mention him and the forgetful forget his mention. And may blessings be upon the messengers. And praise is to Allah, the Lord of the worlds.

BIBLIOGRAPHY

[الْمَصَادِرُ]

al-ʿAjlūnī, Ismāʿīl bin Muḥammad. Cairo: Maktabat al-Qudsī, 1351.

al-Anṣārī, Zakariyyā. *Asnā al-maṭālib*. Beirut: Al-Maktab al-Islāmī, n.d.

al-Asfahānī, Abū Nuʿaym. *Ḥilyat al-awliyāʾ*. Cairo: Al-Saʿādah, 1974/1394.

al-Ashʿarī, Abū Ḥasan. *Maqālāt al-islāmiyyīn*. n.p.: Al-Maktabah al-ʿAṣriyyah, 1426/2005.

al-ʿAsqalānī, Ibn Ḥajar, and Muḥammad ibn Ismāʿīl al-Bukhārī. *Fatḥ al-Bārī bi sharḥ Ṣaḥīḥ al-Bukhārī*. Edited by Muḥammad Fuʿād ʿAbd al-Bāqī and Muḥibb al-Dīn al-Khaṭīb. Cairo: Maktabat al-Salafiyya, 1390/1970.

———. *Al-Talkhīṣ al-ḥabīr*. Egypt: Muʾassisah Quṭibah, 1995/1416.

Abū Dāwūd, Sulaymān bin al-Ashʿath al-Sajisānī. *Al-Sunan* ("Abū Dāwūd"). Edited by Muḥammad Muḥya al-Dīn ʿAbd al-Ḥamīd. Beirut: Dār al-Fikr, n.d.

al-Bayhaqī, Abū Bakr. *Al-Biʿth wa al-nushūr*. Beirut: Markaz al-Khidamāt wa-l-Abḥāth, 1986/1406.

———. *Dalāʾil al-nabuwwah*. Beirut: Dār al-Kutub al-ʿIlmiyyah, 1405.

———. *Shuʿab al-īmān* ("al-Bayhaqī)". Edited by ʿAbd al-ʿAlī ʿAbd al-Ḥamīd, et al. Riyadh: Maktabat al-Rushd, 2003/1423.

al-Bayjūri, Ibrāhīm. *Tuḥfat al-murīd ʿalā Jawharat al-tawḥīd* ("*Jawharah*"). Edited by Ali Gomaa. Cairo: Dār al-Salām, 2002/1422. (Note: "al-Bayjūrī" and "al-Bājūrī" are both correct.)

al-Bukhārī, Muḥammad bin Ismāʿīl Abū ʿAbd Allāh. *Al-Jāmiʿ al-ṣaḥīḥ al-mukhtaṣar min umūr rasūli Llāh* ﷺ wa sunanihi wa ayyāmihi (*Ṣaḥīḥ al-Bukhārī*) ("al-Bukhārī"). Edited by Muḥammad Zuhayr bin Nāṣir al-Nāṣir. n.a.: Dār Tawq al-Najāh, 1422 AH.

al-Dhahabī, Shams al-Dīn. *Siyar aʿlām al-nubalāʾ*. Cairo: Dār al-Ḥadīth, 2006/1427.

al-Ghazālī, Abū Ḥāmid. *Iḥyāʾ ʿulūm al-dīn*. Dār al-Maʿrifah, n.d..

al-Ḥākim, Abū ʿAbd Allāh Muḥammad. *Al-Mustadrak ʿalā al-Ṣaḥīḥayn* ("al-Ḥākim"). Edited by Muṣṭafā ʿAbd al-Qādir ʿAṭā. Beirut: Dār al-Kutub al-ʿIlmiyyah, 1990/1411.

Ibn ʿAsākir. *Tārīkh Dimashq*. Beirut: Dār al-Fikr, 1995/1415.

Ibn Ḥanbal, Aḥmed. *Al-Musnad* ("Aḥmad"). Edited by Shuʿayb al-Arnāʾūṭ, ʿĀdil Murshid, et al. Beirut: Muʾassisah al-Risālah, 2001/1421.

Ibn Ḥibbān, Muḥammad al-Bustī and al-Amīr ʿAlāʾ al-Dīn ʿAlī bin Balbān al-Fārasī. *Al-Iḥsān fī taqrīb Ṣaḥīḥ Ibn Ḥibbān* ("Ibn Ḥibbān"). Edited by Shūʿayb al-Arnāʾūṭ. ʿAmmān: Muʾassisat al-Risālah, 1988/1408.

Ibn Mājah, Abū ʿAbd Allāh Muḥammad bin Yazīd al-Qizwīnī. *Sunan Ibn Mājah* ("Ibn Mājah"). Edited by Muḥammad Fūʾād ʿAbd al-Bāqī. Aleppo: Dār Iḥyāʾ al-Kutub al-ʿArabiyyah, n.d.

Ibn al-Mulaqqin. *Tuḥfat al-muḥtāj*. Beirut: Al-Maktabah al-Islāmiyyah, 1994.

al-ʿIrāqī, Zayn al-Dīn. *Takhrīj aḥādīth Iḥyāʾ ʿulūm al-dīn*. Beirut: Dār Ibn Ḥazm, 2005/1426.

al-Jāwī, Muḥammad Nawawī al-Bantanī. *Al-Thimār al-yāniʿ*. Beirut: Dār al-Kutub al-ʿIlmiyyah, 2013/1434.

———. *Tījān al-darādīr*. Printed within *Majmūʿ shams rasāʾil fī l-ʿaqāʾid*. Amman: Dār al-nūr al-mubīn, 2013.

al-Mubārakfūrī, ʿAbd al-Raḥmān. *Al-Tuḥfat al-aḥwadhī*. Beirut: Dār al-Kutub al-ʿIlmiyyah, 1353.

Muslim bin al-Ḥajjāj. *Al-Musnad al-ṣaḥīḥ al-mukhtaṣar bi-naql al-'adl 'an al-'adl ilā rasūl Allāh* ﷺ ("Muslim"). Edited by Muḥammad Fu'ād 'Abd al-Bāqī. Beirut: Dār Iḥyā' al-Turāth, n.d.

al-Nasā'ī, Abū 'Abd al-Raḥmān Aḥmed bin Shu'ayb. *Al-Mujtabā* ("al-Nasā'ī"). Edited by 'Abd al-Fattāḥ Abū Ghuddah, 2nd ed. Aleppo: Maktab al-Maṭbū'āt al-Islāmiyyah, n.d.

———. *Al-Sunan al-kubrā*. Edited by 'Abd al-Ghaffār Sulaymān al-Bandārī. Beirut: Dār al-Kutub al-'Ilmiyyah, n.d.

al-Nawawī, Ibrāhīm bin Sharaf. *Kitāb al-adhkār*. Dār Ibn Ḥazm, 2004/1425.

———. *Al-Minhāj sharḥ Ṣaḥīḥ Muslim bin al-Hajjāj*. Beirut: Dār Iḥyā' al-Turāth al-'Arabī, 1392.

———. *Rawḍat al-ṭālibīn*. Beirut: Al-Maktab al-Islāmī, 1991/1412.

al-Qārī, Mullā 'Alī. *Mirqāt al-mafātīḥ sharḥ Moshkāt al-maṣābīḥ*. Lebanon: Dar al-Fikr, 2002/1422.

al-Qurṭubī, Shams al-Dīn. *Al-Tadhkirah bi aḥwāl al-mawt*. Riyāḍ: Dār al-Minhāj, 1425.

al-Sha'rānī, 'Abd al-Wahhāb. *Al-Minaḥ al-saniyyah 'alā Al-Waṣiyyah al-Maṭbūliyyah*.

al-Shirbīnī, al-Khaṭīb. *Al-Sirāj al-Munīr*. Cairo: Bulāq, 1285.

———. *Mughnī al-muḥtāj*. Beirut: Dār al-Kutub al-'Ilmiyyah, 1994/1415.

al-Sulamī, Abū 'Abd al-Raḥmān. *Ṭabaqāt al-ṣūfiyyah*. Beirut: Dār al-Kutub al-'Ilmiyyah, 1997/1419.

al-Suyūṭī. *Jāmi' al-aḥādīth*. Cairo: n.p., 2002/1423.

———. *Jam' al-jawāmi'*. Cairo: al-Azhar al-Sharīf, 2005/1426.

———. *Al-Jāmi' al-ṣaghīr*. N.p: Al-Maktabah al-Shāmilah, n.d.

———. *Al-Tawshīḥ sharḥ Al-Jāmi' al-ṣaḥīḥ*. Riyāḍ: Maktabat al-Rushd, 1998/1419.

al-Ṭabarānī, Sulaymān bin Aḥmed bin Ayyūb bin Muṭīr. *Al-Mu'jam al-kabīr*. Edited by Ḥamdī al-Salafī, 2nd ed. n.a.: Maktabat al-'Ulūm wa-l-Ḥikam, n.d.

al-Tirmidhī, Muḥammad bin ʿĪsā bin Sawrah bin Mūsā. *Al-Sunan* ("al-Tirmidhī"). Edited by Aḥmed Muḥammad Shākir, et al, 2nd edition. Cairo: Sharikah Maktabah wa Maṭbaʿah Muṣṭafā al-Bābī al-Ḥalabī, 1975/1395.

al-ʿUqaylī, Abū Jaʿfar. *Al-Ḍuʿafāʾ al-kabīr.* Beirut: Dār al-Kutub al-ʿIlmiyyah, 1984/1404.

DETAILED TABLE OF CONTENTS

المُحْتَوَيَاتُ المُفَصَّلَةُ

Also from Islamosaic

Ark of Salvation

Connecting to the Quran

Etiquette with the Quran

Infamies of the Soul

Hadith Nomenclature Primers

Hanbali Acts of Worship

Ibn Juzay's Sufic Exegesis

Refutation of Those Who Do Not Follow the Four Schools

Sharḥ Al-Waraqāt

Shaykh al-Sulamī's Waṣiyyah

Supplement for the Seeker of Certitude

The Accessible Conspectus

The Encompassing Epistle

The Evident Memorandum

The Ladder to Success

The Ultimate Conspectus

Printed in Great Britain
by Amazon

18434110R00079